MIDAS' DAUGHTER TURNED TO GOLD

GODS
AND
GODDESSES

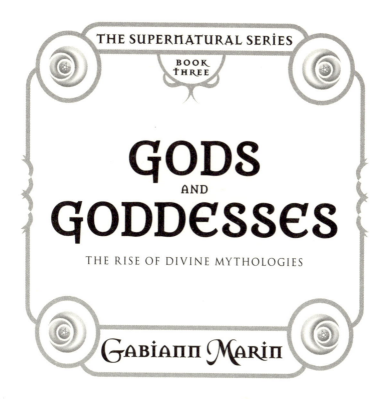

THE SUPERNATURAL SERIES

BOOK THREE

GODS
AND
GODDESSES

THE RISE OF DIVINE MYTHOLOGIES

Gabiann Marin

ROCKPOOL
PUBLISHING

This book is dedicated to my dear nephew, Ziggy, whose
birthday I missed while writing it. He's a writer …
he understands …

A Rockpool book
PO Box 252
Summer Hill
NSW 2130
Australia
www.rockpoolpublishing.com.au
http://www.facebook.com/RockpoolPublishing

First published in 2017
Copyright text © Gabiann Marin 2017
Copyright Design © Rockpool Publishing 2017
This edition published in 2017

National Library of Australia Cataloguing-in-Publication entry

Creator: Marin, Gabiann, author.
Title: Gods and goddesses / Gabiann Marin.
ISBN: 9781925017472 (hardback)
Series: Marin, Gabiann, Supernatural ; 3
Subjects: Gods.
Mythology.
Mythology, Classical.

Cover design by Seymour Design
Cover artwork by Amalia Chitulescu
Cover images by Shutterstock
Front Endpapers: Thor (Johannes Gehrts 1901), The Midas Myth (Walter Crane 1893),
    The Rhinegold & The Valkyrie (Arthur Rackham 1910)
Back Endpapers: The Midas Myth (Walter Crane 1893), Freya in Dwarfs' Cave (Huard
    1891), Thor (Johannes Gehrts 1901)
Typesetting by Typeskill
Printed and bound in China

10 9 8 7 6 5 4 3 2 1

Contents

❧

Introduction   1

1. **The Creation of the Gods**   3
The Sun, the Moon and the Earth

2. **The Ancient Ones**   13
The Gods and Goddesses of Mesopotamia

3. **Divine Royalty**   35
The Gods and Goddesses of Egypt

4. **Haven't I Seen You Somewhere Before?**   51
The Greco-Roman Pantheon

5. **Gods in a Rational World**   69
The Gods and Goddesses of Ancient China

6. **The Warriors in the Sky**   87
The Norse Gods and Goddesses

7. **Nature Spirits**   105
The Celtic Divinities

8. **Don't Disappoint Us!**   125
The Gods and Goddesses of Pre-Columbian
America

9. **The Voodoo You Do So Well**   141
West Africa and the Voodoo Loa

10. **Modern Gods**   161

Introduction

If God didn't exist, we would have to invent him.

Voltaire

❧

GODS AND goddesses have been part of human evolution. They have provided us with knowledge, meaning and a sense of place within a vast, frightening universe. Many gods and goddesses have fulfilled these roles over the ages, each with their own specific role and personality. Some have been kind and gentle, others terrifying. Some took the form of the impressive natural landmarks around us, while others manifested themselves in the guise of animals or animal hybrids. Many took on the form of human beings and reflected us.

However we imagined them, their role was the same; to help explain the unknown, offer protection and create a sense of community — often within a hostile land.

As we built cities and civilisations, launched ourselves across the seas and later up into the stars, our understanding of these gods changed. Some migrated with us into the 21st century while others seemingly abandoned us in the ruins of time.

But regardless of their current status, every god and goddess who has ever been worshipped has left their mark on human endeavour and, even those we may think long forgotten, still exist with us in our stories and our language.

This book will introduce you to the great deities of the ancient world. How they shaped the world around us, how they were loved and worshipped and how they still live on with us, in our language, our practices, our science and even our spiritual lives.

Modern culture owes much to those who once were worshipped and their immortality is still influential, incorporated into everything from scientific and medical jargon, popular television shows, medicine, entertainment and even capitalist business culture.

So come with me on a journey to meet and remember the gods and goddesses of old. I have no doubt they will both horrify and delight, amaze and inspire and perhaps even help you connect to the universal consciousness from which all deities have emerged.

CHAPTER ONE

The Creation of the Gods

The Sun, the Moon and the Earth

❧

THE SUN has been a centrepiece of many of the great ancient religions. It has been imagined as a mighty warrior, carrying a torch through the sky as it chased its lost love, the Moon goddess, destined never to catch her as it plunged into the waters of the horizon. Some saw it as a youth in a great chariot, pulled by fiery horses in a great race to beat time itself. Others saw it as a hard, weary worker, trudging its way homewards every day across the sky.

Whatever the stories, the Sun was seen as both benign and wrathful. It rarely thought of, or cared for, those who depended upon its light and warmth down on Earth. Yet it always had a purpose, a personality, a story to explain its endless cycles across the sky.

❧

One of the earliest stories of the Sun god concerns the son of the Moon goddess, who was determined to make his own way in the world.

He did not heed his mother's warnings and left her side, leaving her world in darkest grief as he travelled across the heavens. Yet his way was harder than he imagined, and being young and impetuous, he decided to stop his travels and sit high in the sky, his great fire burning with immortal light.

With no respite from the heat of the Sun god's light the great rivers and lakes receded into the oceans to shelter from the heat. Without water and unable to protect themselves from the great heat the animals and people thirsted and burned.

The animals and people decided they must go to the great ocean and ask for its help, as the only thing that the young Sun god feared was the waters of life.

The ocean listened to the people and the animals and considered their request. Usually she was peaceful but she had grown angry from the attacks on her children of the inlands and so she mustered up a great storm, which swept the Sun god out of the sky and extinguished the fiery light of his soul.

The Sun god however, was not willing to give up his sky dominion so easily and although he retreated for a time, he returned and a great battle raged. The ocean sent up a huge storm of water into the sky, to be fought by the Sun with shafts of purest white light and deafening roars of thunder.

Eventually the Sun triumphed and the storm would return back into the calm waters of the sea, and the people, also buffeted and decimated by the storm, would welcome back the Sun, forgetting the reason for the storm in the first place.

But the Sun again took up his position and the waters again receded and the people again suffered and the Ocean's wrath erupted with rain and thunder. The world was awash and then burned as the great Sun and the powerful Ocean fought on and on.

The people and the animals regretted their request to the ocean and worried at how to end the great war that now raged above them. Then a wise woman looked up into the sky and saw the Moon peeking through the clouds. 'Oh great goddess Moon, mother of the Sun, can you not help us end this terrible conflict?'

The Moon looked down on the people and she took pity on them. She had seen how this conflict had ravaged the Earth, her great silent mother, and she knew she must do something to stop it.

She called a meeting with her child and the Ocean goddess and the three great deities sat down and presented their arguments.

'My home is the sky, you cannot keep me from it,' the Sun god declared.

'I do not wish to own the sky, but your great fire burns the land and my lakes and rivers cannot feed the Earth and those upon it', the Ocean goddess responded.

The Moon mother listened to the two sides and suggested a compromise.

'My son, if you stay in the sky forever the Earth will burn, the people will die and you will be alone. Instead move across the sky and spread your light. Then give the great Ocean your flame at the end of each journey for the Earth and you to rest.'

The Ocean agreed that she would accept this. But the Sun god was not convinced, 'if the water of the Ocean swallows me the great light will be extinguished, I will be lost and then who shall light the Earth and warm the sky?', he asked.

'I will,' his mother replied. 'I will come and watch over the earth during the times you are away. And I will keep a spark of your great light with me, to ensure that it cannot be completely extinguished by the great Ocean. Once the Earth has rested I will give you the spark and you can again light your great torch and move across the sky.'

And so it was decided and the Sun moved across the sky each day, and each night it was swallowed by the great ocean. The Moon, holding the sacred spark, travelled along the sky after her son, to relight his great light and rebirth him.

༺࿔༻

This story is a re-telling of several of the great Sun myths from multiple early religions – all of which feature different characters who undertake the same basic functions in order to help explain the dawning and setting of the Sun and the cycles of the seasons.

As early people were reliant on understanding the movement of the Sun and the timings of spring, winter, summer and autumn in order to prepare for times of deprivation and times of plenty, it is hardly surprising that they were so interested in the powers which might determine these cycles, and imagined they could be appealed to in times of extreme weather conditions.

The Sun God - The Son Of God

Theologians and scholars of comparative religion have made a strong case that the Christian story of Jesus Christ has many similarities with the ancient stories of the Sun gods. The focus on resurrection in the New Testament reflects the resurrection of the Sun and the explanation of changing seasons used across ancient and modern sun worship.

In all religions where a Sun god became a prime deity, their story incorporated some form of resurrection – including the stories of the Egyptian Sun god Osiris and the Mesopotamian Sun god, Mithras; both of them represent the death and rebirth of the Sun.

Brother Sun – Sister Moon?

Across most religions the Sun god was seen as a male deity, usually with a female consort or mother who represented

Cosmos, Flammarion Woodcut

the Moon or the Ocean. The female companion was usually
instrumental in the resurrection of the Sun god and the
connection to the emotional depth and compassion of
the Moon and water was established quite early because
of this association.

However there were a few notable female Sun goddesses
even in the earliest religions. The Mesopotamian/Sumerian
religion worshipped the goddess Arinna, who was herself
based on the Hittite goddess of the Sun, Hepa.

In ancient Japanese mythology the most important
deity was Amaterasu, a Sun goddess, and the Norse

religion associated the warrior goddess Freya with the Sun and the heavens.

The Setting of the Sun

As civilisations became more conversant with the movement of the Sun and the changing of the seasons, the Sun gods and goddesses started to lose prevalence in their religions. In later religions the most important gods and goddesses would connect more closely with the main concern of the culture, many becoming gods and goddesses of the heavens or the Earth.

Mother Earth

As nature and the natural changes in the environment were such a strong source of religious worship and focus, it is hardly surprising that the Earth herself became an important deity in most civilisations. Yet for all her importance she was mainly a passive force in the mythologies of the different cultures. In personality she was seen as loving and nurturing, but essentially willing to sit back and allow the more extroverted gods and goddesses to play out their dramas on the stages she provided.

Called by many names: Gaia, Maya, Tonantzin, Antum, Panchamama; the concept of a deity that covered the entire planet was a later development. More commonly in individual worship the Earth mother was perceived as

several different deities who governed over specific natural formations and cycles.

In Hawaii, the creator goddess Pele was signified by a volcano, in Nepal, Chomolungma, now commonly known as Mount Everest, was seen as a mother goddess to the Nepalese people. The Aztecs revered Panchamama, who personified earthquakes, and was represented as the Andes mountains. Other civilisations saw the Earth mother as more metaphorical, representing forests, harvests, spring, and oceans as well as specific rock and terrestrial formations.

Today the echoes of the Earth goddess can be found in our term Mother Nature which is a modern version of the Gaia, Mother Earth concept.

The traditional reference to land as female, such as Mother Land and Mother Country, as well as referring to the language of our origin country as our Mother Tongue is another way the concept of a mother goddess connected to the land is carried through into modern times.

CHAPTER TWO

The Ancient Ones

THE GODS AND GODDESSES OF MESOPOTAMIA

❦

LONG BEFORE all memory. Before the great Roman Empire rose under the gaze of Jupiter and Juno, or the Aztec gods demanded sacrifices from a blood ritual. Before even the Egyptian Pharaohs worshipped Nut and Ra as the universal sky and earth; there was a world overseen by two powerful female goddesses. Inanna and her elder sister Ereshkigal held the people of Sumer in their powerful grip.

❦

The two sisters did not get along. Inanna found Eriskahal to be petty and jealous, and Ereshkigal thought Inanna proud and arrogant. For many years the other Sumerian gods tolerated the rivalry of the sisters, fearful of showing a favourite – for although, as different as night and day, both goddesses were equally fearsome.

But the two women could not live together in the divine realm and eventually it was decreed by the Sumerian gods that Inanna, as goddess of love and war, would rule the Earth and skies and Ereshkigal would reside over the misty realm of Irkallah, as the all-powerful queen of the underworld.

Ereshkigal was far from happy with this arrangement but was placated when she realised that there was no greater power than that of death and so she accepted the arrangement and took the title of 'The Lady of the Great Place'. She and her beloved husband, The Bull of the Heavens, took up residence in Irkallah, the underworld in the land of Kur, while her younger sister took up her position in the heavens.

The sisters remained quiet and content in their own realms, although occasionally they would hear word of one another and wonder if the other was happier or more celebrated than they.

Then one day the god of wisdom, Enki, decided to give Inanna the power of the universal laws. Ereshkigal, hearing of this, was furious. This was a clear sign that she had been forgotten in her underworld lair.

But before she could fully respond to this new development King Gilgamesh's henchman murdered Ereshkigal's husband, and her rage and grief overtook all else.

The force of her pain and anger caused earthquakes and landslides. The gods of Sumer were alarmed, as they remembered how dangerous the goddess Ereshkigal could be.

'She is in mourning,' Inanna told her servant, Ninshubar. 'Fetch me my armour and my jewels, for I should go down into the underworld and see my sister in her time of need.'

The maidservant, knowing how fierce the rivalry was between the two sisters, begged Inanna not to go, but Inanna would not listen and bade Ninshubar to get her ready for the journey.

Over her rich, royal robes Inanna layered gleaming armour, hammered out of the finest gold and heavy with jewels. She looked at her image in the mirror and, deciding she needed more finery, she decked herself in gold and diamond rings and beads of finest lapis. She picked up a jewel-encrusted staff and placed the great crown of heaven upon her head. Satisfied she turned to her maidservant and declared herself ready to journey to the Sumerian land of the dead.

'No one returns from the land of the Kur, m'lady,' Ninshubar cautioned. 'It is not wise to go there, even if the queen Ereshkigal is your sister.'

Inanna dismissed her servant's protests, throwing back her head arrogantly, her golden locks rippling across her shoulders. 'How can I rule over the universal laws of the universe if I have never seen death?' Inanna responded. 'Do not worry, my armour and robes are enchanted and no harm will come to me.' Ninshubar knew there was no point arguing with Inanna, so instead she insisted that her lady take all caution, then bade her farewell.

Inanna travelled down into the depths of the Earth, the pathway lit by a few spluttering torches. Once she saw the great gates of Kur she knew she had arrived.

The door opened a crack and a dark, shrouded face peered at her from beyond the gate. 'I cannot let you pass. This is a place for the dead, not the living,' declared the gatekeeper, Neti, slamming the gate shut in the goddess's face.

Inanna banged impatiently. 'I have come to see my sister Ereshkigal. I am Inanna, queen of the sky. She will see me.'

Through the door he called to her gruffly. 'Wait here. I shall see if the Queen is willing to allow you entrance.'

In the great cavern of Ereshkigal's underworld palace, Neti rushed to speak with the queen.

'Your sister comes, she is waiting at the first gateway.'

Ereshkigal, dressed in a sackcloth of mourning, her red eyes ringed with grief, looked at her servant in surprise. 'Why does she come? Is she here to try and comfort me? Mourn with me the death of my great love?'

Neti shook his head, 'she is not dressed in mourning clothes,she wears great jewels, golden armour and silken, colourful robes'.

Ereshkigal's anger rose, her sister was here in her finery, while Ereshkigal wore ashes and sackcloth? The arrogance!

'I can forbid her entrance,' Neti said, preparing to go back to the Sky goddess and refuse her request. Ereshkigal

bit her lip and considered
what to do. Denying her
sister entry was her right
as Queen of Irkallah, but
perhaps it was better to
allow her sister in. After
all, once in the kingdom of
the dead, it was Ereshkigal's
power that was greater.

'No, no we cannot
be so inhospitable to my
dear sister. She wants to
come and experience the
world of the dead, we shall
let her.'

Neti frowned, unsure
what the queen was
planning.

'However as she enters
each gateway you must
take one item from her, as a
token of her reverence.'

Inanna had grown
impatient by the time
Neti returned and rapped
on the gate imperiously.
Neti smiled and bowed,

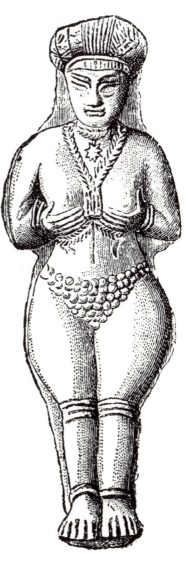

opening the heavy door so Inanna could see the almost impenetrable abyss beyond.

'The great Ereshkigal has agreed to an audience,' he advised her. 'But in order to pass through these gates you must give me your crown.'

Inanna was surprised, but seeing no harm she handed the crown over to Neti, who expertly hid it away in the folds of his robe. They walked into the inky darkness until another gate appeared before them.

'I must ask for your beads,' Neti said. Inanna resisted, her beads were precious, a gift from her husband Dumazai.

'You must make an offering at every gate to enter the land of the dead,' Neti insisted. Inanna reluctantly removed the beads and they also disappeared within Neti's mysterious robe.

At each gate Neti took another item from Inanna, her rings, then her staff, her armour and finally her beautiful royal clothes.

They got to the last of the great gates and Inanna had nothing left to give. Neti just smiled at her darkly and allowed her entrance.

'What? There is no toll for this gate?' Inanna asked.

'There is always a price, m'lady'. Neti replied, ushering Inanna inside and through to where Ereshkigal sat in her mourning clothes.

Inanna, naked and vulnerable, still had her pride and stood up straight and regally in front of Ereshkigal.

'Why do you come here?' Ereshkigal asked.

Inanna shrugged. 'I heard you crying, and I thought I should see what could so upset the Queen of the Night.'

Ereshkigal frowned. 'I have lost my husband.'

'But surely you must be used to death, being surrounded by it,' Inanna remarked thoughtlessly.

A dark shadow clouded Ereshkigal's face and her lips pulled back into a snarl. Inanna, oblivious to the danger, looked around the cavern and shivered at the cold dankness.

'This really is an awful place …'

But before she could finish her sentence Ereshkigal struck her down with the look of death, killing Inanna instantly.

'Now you too will know what it is like to be surrounded only by the dead,' Ereshkigal said as she gestured for her servants to gather up Inanna's corpse and hang it from some hooks and chains in the corner of the room.

In the heavenly kingdom Ninshubar awaited Inanna's return. Three days and three nights passed with not a word and the girl got increasingly worried. Eventually having heard nothing on the fourth day, Ninshubar sought out Dumazai, Inanna's husband, and told him of her concerns.

'I have no power in the underworld,' Dumazai replied. 'There is nothing I can do if she was so foolish as to venture there. It seems she is lost to us.' And then instead of mourning, as Ninshubar had expected, Dumazai drank deeply from his wine goblet and declared 'But life goes on.'

Ninshubar refused to give up and asked Nanna, the
god of the Moon and Enil the god of the air, to help
her retrieve Inanna from the underworld. But both gods
refused, knowing that once one enters the underworld, it is
forbidden to ever return.

Finally, not knowing who else to turn to, Ninshubar
visited Enki, god of wisdom and water.

'You must help her,' Ninshubar pleaded. 'You gave her
the gift of the universal laws and if she is dead, then the
great laws will surely die with her.'

Enki knew the truth of these words and agreed to help.
He considered for a moment and then dug the earth from
beneath his fingernails, and fashioned two magical creatures
— the Galla, who he gave to Ninshubar.

'These creatures can take on any shape. Give them the
waters and food of life to take down to Inanna so that she
may be resurrected.'

Ninshubar did as she was told and the Galla turned
themselves into flies and crawled through the cracks in
the earth and into the depths of the underworld. They
were able to slip through the seven gates of Kur without
alerting Neti and fly soundlessly into the throne room of
Queen Ereshkigal.

The creatures saw Inanna's broken body hanging from
hooks in the throne room and hastened their way towards
the dead goddess, but were stopped in their tracks by the
sound of weeping and moaning coming from the throne.

There Queen Ereshkigal sat sobbing, alone and uncared for. Being kindly creatures they could not leave such a pitiful woman without comfort. They flew towards her, transforming themselves into beings of warm light and embraced Ereshkigal, echoing her cries as she mourned her husband.

Ereshkigal looked up at these beings and felt their compassion and kindness, something which she had craved but not received since the death of her dearest husband. Her head felt clear and her pain lifted. Sorrow started to diminish and her heart felt light.

'You are kind and good creatures. You have given me that which none other has offered me, as such I shall offer you whatever you desire.'

The two creatures kissed away Ereshkigal's tears and then told her they had come for the body of Inanna, which hung in the throne room.

Ereshkigal looked at her sister's remains, and nodded. She could not deny the Galla their request and they quickly enveloped the dead goddess, unchaining her from the wall and placing her gently on the floor of the cavern. One Galla carefully lifted Inanna's head while the other fed her the food of life and made her sip from the cup of immortality.

Inanna awoke from her death and looked around the room, feeling the warmth of the creatures around her. 'You have saved me? But who sent you? My husband?'

'We come from the god Enki, your servant Ninshubar did not give up on you and convinced him to help you return to us.'

Inanna got unsteadily to her feet. 'And my husband Dumazai, did he also demand my return?'

The creatures looked away, not wanting to reveal the truth to the goddess. But she saw it anyway — her husband had not grieved her death. Ereshkigal watched her sister with pained eyes. 'I cannot let Inanna leave the underworld, despite my promise. It is the universal law, which Inanna herself is sworn to uphold.'

Inanna nodded and stood up, addressing her sister. 'I was arrogant and foolish to come here. I knew the laws and felt myself above them. I did not comfort you in your mourning, but instead wished only to exert my own power over life and death. The grief you have for your husband is real, yet my husband does not mourn me. Your love is truly greater than mine. I shall stay here and make a home in Irkallah.'

The creatures fluttered about the room, unsure how to fulfil their mission, but they knew it was hopeless, despite their best efforts.

Ereshkigal stepped forward. 'There is one way …'

Dumazai swallowed the grape, which had been passed to him by a delectable young woman, one of many who currently lazed around his gardens. As the god of the harvest he was a popular figure to the Sumerians, who were happy to provide him with whatever luxuries he desired.

'Brother, you are being disrespectful to Inanna!'
Dumazai's sister, Geshtinanna scolded as she placed a bowl
of food in front of him. 'You should be wearing sackcloth
and mourning like her servants and the other gods.'

Dumazai shrugged his shoulders, he knew he should
feel worse about her passing, but with so many distractions
it was difficult to stay unhappy for long. 'She is dead, what
care she if I enjoy the long days of summer instead of
surrounding myself in sorrow?', he asked, popping some
dried figs into his mouth.

'I care much more than you may believe, dear husband.'

Dumazai, almost choking on his food, spun himself
around on his chair to see Inanna standing at the gateway
of the garden. Standing next to her was a tall, dark-winged
woman, wearing a dress of ashen sackcloth and holding a staff
of ebony black. He knew instantly that this was Inanna's older
sister, the terrifying Queen of the Underworld, Ereshkigal.

'Inanna! I thought you dead!', he stumbled to his feet and
knelt before her.

She waved him away, and turned to her sister, 'You will
accept him as my _____ ent?'

Ereshki_____ ____ed and raised her staff to club Dumazai
acro___ ___ head. Geshtinanna, realising her brother's peril
rushed forward.

'No, please, do not take him. He is young and foolish
but he is needed for the harvest. If he dies the crops die
with him.'

Ereshkigal, unmoved, swung the staff downwards, but it was stopped by Inanna's strong grip.

'She is right. The people have already suffered with my passing. We cannot let them starve because he is not here to bless their crops.'

Ereshkigal pulled back the staff. 'You have chosen Dumazai, you do not get another choice. It is not my fault if you chose in error.'

'No, please, please,' Geshtinanna begged, 'take me instead.'

The two goddesses looked at Geshtinanna, and then at Dumazai. 'Yes, take her,' he cried, grabbing his sister and pushing her towards Ereshkigal. 'She is not an important deity. She will not be missed.'

Inanna took the staff from Ereshkigal and cracked Dumazai across the head. 'Your sister is a better soul than you ever were. She is willing to sacrifice herself for you, yet you sacrifice for no one!'

Dumazai writhed on the ground in pain from the blow, as Geshtinanna tried to tend to his injury. Inanna turned to her sister, 'Can you take Dumazai but release him for part of the year to bless the crops and allow the people to harvest?'

Ereshkigal considered this. 'I will allow the people one great season of harvesting per year. During that time I will take the girl as Dumazai's replacement, but if he fails to return, my wrath will be swift and he will be bound in Irkallah for all time.'

Geshtinanna got to her feet and thanked Ereshkigal, who shook her head and pulled away. 'He is a stupid and frivolous man, he does not deserve the gift you have given him.'

'He is my brother, no matter what his flaws, I must love and keep him safe. That is what family does for one another.'

Inanna and Ereshkigal glanced at each other, seeing the other's shame at how they had quarrelled and harmed each other. They were both moved by Geshtinanna's sacrifice for her brother and in that moment knew that although they would always be rivals, they could also be friends.

～

The Descent of Inanna is one of the most famous of all the Sumerian myths and forms one of the great stories in the epic poem *Gilgamesh*. Its central idea, that of descending into the afterlife and the price to return, has been reflected in many of the later myths and legends, like Hades and Persephone in Greece, Isis and Osiris in Egypt and even the resurrection stories of the Old and New Testament.

The land of Mesopotamia stretched across the Middle East into Asia Minor and the top of North Africa between 5000 BCE until 1070 BCE. This vast expanse included the empires of the Hittites, the Assyrians, the Babylonians and the Sumerians who occupied different parts of the regions throughout these times. The Mesopotamian gods and goddesses were particularly resilient, many surviving each new invasion and adopted into their new culture with little more than a change of name.

Because of the size of this region and the individual tribal elements of each of the cultures, there is estimated to have been over 1000 Mesopotamian gods and goddesses who were worshipped across this area. Some were specific to a particular natural landmark, such as lakes and rivers, but many more were simply slightly different versions of the same deities adopted under new names.

The most well known of all these deities is the goddess Isthar, also known as Astarte and Inanna, across the region. A Sky goddess known for her beauty, in her Ishtar form she was also known as a seductress who regularly intervened in the affairs of Assyrian kings, most notably the King Gilgamesh whose tale was told in the epic poem titled after him.

Ishtar was originally conceived in the first of the Mesopotamian cultures, the Sumer empire in 5000 BCE, as the Sky goddess Inanna, a much less sexualised goddess than her later Assyrian version, but equally powerful and beloved.

Ereshkigal is the first known representation of a strong female death god, and is reflected by female underworld goddesses in Norse and Celtic religions. The Greek underworld goddess Persephone, whose legend strongly mirrors that of the descent of Inanna, is seen as merely a

consort of the underworld god Hades, yet she is arguably a more powerful figure in the myths of the Greek underworld than her husband as it is she, not him, who takes some of the key actions in the great underworld myths.

The 1986 Hollywood film *Ghostbusters* based the central villain, a Sumerian deity called Zuul and her henchwoman, Gozer, on several key elements of the goddess Ereshkigal.

In the film Zuul possesses an innocent woman and makes her a powerful, vengeful goddess, complete with two shapeshifting minions similar to the Galla in the original myth. *Ghostbusters*, like so much of popular culture today has sexualised and demonised the once powerful ancient goddesses, ignoring the complexity of their original stories.

The Epic of 'Gilgamesh'

Most of what we know about the Sumerian gods and goddesses comes from the epic poem *Gilgamesh* written in the 18th century BCE. The poem was recovered on twelve stone tablets, and follows the adventures and travails of the fictional Sumerian king.

The main narrative concerns the adventures of the cruel King as he is smitten by the gods and forced to wander in exile until his death. He searches for immortality and finds the one human, Utnapishtim, upon whom the god Enil granted the gift of everlasting life. Like so many of the great epic poems which would follow, such as *The Iliad* and *The Odyssey* by Homer, *Gilgamesh* tells the story of a journey by an extraordinary human who encounters the gods and goddesses, making friends and enemies along the way.

'Gilgamesh' and Noah's Ark

The biblical Old Testament story of Noah's Ark owes much to the epic of *Gilgamesh*. The biblical story describes how an old man, Noah, is told by God of an impending flood and instructed to build a great ship in which to house and protect one mating pair of each animal to ensure that life can continue after the flood.

In the epic of *Gilgamesh* when the king finally finds Utnapishtim he learns that the man earned immortality by building a huge raft on which to survive a great flood which was created by the god Enil after he was disgusted with the stupidity of humankind.

The storm lasts for six days and nights after which Utnapishtim, his raft lodged on the top of a mountain, releases a dove, a raven and a swallow to find out if the gods have left any dry land for him to rebuild the human race.

When the raven does not return Utnapishtim takes this as a sign that it is safe to release the inhabitants of the raft.

Although the point of the story in *Gilgamesh* is in the gaining of immortality by Utnapishtim, this is lost in the biblical retelling of the story, which focuses more on Noah saving the animals. In the story of Noah's Ark the outcome is not personal immortality but rather the survival of mankind and all the animal species.

The biblical story also makes reference to the use of a dove and a raven, although for some reason the swallow is not incorporated into the biblical tale.

Rituals and Worship in Ancient Mesopotamia

The people of Mesopotamia are remembered today as the creators of civilisation. They established cities, created art and culture, farmed and produced goods for trade and leisure. The first recorded writings of the Sumer people date around 3500 BCE. As such the rituals and worship of their deities was the first to be comprehensively documented.

The deities were highly important to the daily lives of the Sumerians, as well as the later Hittites, Babylonians, Akkadians and Assyrians who adopted the gods and goddesses. Known collectively as the Mesopotamians, these civilisations created elaborate temples called Ziggurats, each dedicated to a different deity.

Offerings and sacrifices were usually in the form of grains, fruits or occasionally meats, which were left at the temples as a gift for the gods in order to gain favour. The Mesopotamians believed that their gods needed to be fed and nourished by their followers and if they were not sated they could become angry and vengeful.

Aside from the daily offering, there were also extra gifts left for the gods during individual celebrations around births and marriages to ensure good luck and protection for the newly born or newlywed.

Funerals also had specific rituals to ensure the timely and safe journey into the underworld by the dead, and included scribing messages or prayers onto the ceramic jars which held the removed organs of the deceased.

There were also a number of annual public festivals — the most important, the Akitu Festival, is the oldest documented New Year's festival, which dates back to 3500 BCE. Based on the turn of the year in the Babylonian calendar (March/April) it was used to celebrate and bless the sowing and cutting of barley crops, an important staple in the region.

There is no doubt that the use of religious festivals and shared holy days, as well as the centralisation of the temples helped to create unity and community within the expanding cities. Without their shared gods, the first civilisations would have been unable to grow as rapidly and effectively as they did.

Important Mesopotamian Deities

Although more than 1000 known gods and goddesses were worshipped across this region, there are a number of key figures who appear across all these cultures, often with slightly different names, who represent the highest order of the Mesopotamian deities.

Name and Region	Rules	Known for
Anu – Babylon **An** – Sumer **Assur** –Assyria	Sky, Lord of heavens, Great Bull, war, Supreme God	The great bull of the sky, his roars were thunder and he snorted lightning.
Enki – Sumer and Akkadia **Ea** – Babylon	Fresh water, wisdom, magic	He defeated his father Apsu and used magic to create the earth

Name and Region	Rules	Known for
Enlil – Sumer	Lord of the air and the wind	Part of the powerful ruling triad with Anu and Enki who ruled the Heavens, Earth and Underworld.
Ereshkigal – Sumer Also known in Babylon, Assyria and Akkadia as: *Lady of the Great Place* *Irkalla* *Queen of the Night*	Goddess of the underworld	Ruled the underworld with her husband the Great Bull.
Erra – Babylon **Nergal** – Assyria	War destruction, death and strife	Features in the epic poem 'Wrath of Erra' where he tricks the god Marduk to leave Babylon and then destroys the city.
Gula – Sumer	Agriculture and healing	A hearth deity mostly worshipped in small regional ceremonies.
Inanna – Sumer **Ishtar** – Babylon **Astarte** – Assyria	Sexuality, passion, fertility, love and war	Continued throughout the Mesopotamian cultures by absorbing the attributes of lesser-known goddesses of other regions.

Name and Region	Rules	Known for
Lamma/ Lammassu – Sumer and Assyria	Both as a female and male – they were deities of protection	Fairly minor gods – well known today because of their numerous carvings and statues used to protect temples and palaces.
Marduk – Sumer and Babylon	King of the Gods	Defeated Tiamat, bringing order to the universe.
Nabu – Babylon	Writing, arts and wisdom	Usually compared to Thoth, Egyptian god of writing and Apollo the Greek god of arts.
Nanna – Sumer **Nanna-Suen** – Babylon **Nannar** – Assyria **Sin** – Assyria	God of full Moon God of creation	Father of Inanna. One of the original gods mentioned in writings of 3500 BCE.
Sherida – Sumer *Serida* **Aja** – Babylon *Aya*	Mother goddess, Sustainer of light and life, goddess of the dawn	Originally a prime deity she later lost popularity. In her incarnation as Aya in Babylon she gained more prestige.

Name and Region	Rules	Known for

Tiamat – Sumer
         Babylon
         Assyria
         Akkadia
	Mother of the gods and primordial mother goddess, chaos	Originally a creator goddess she came to represent chaos and disorder as a dragon defeated by Marduk.

Utu *Shamash* *Samas* *Babbar* - Sumer Babylon, Assyria Akkaria	God of Sun and justice	The first god of the Sun mentioned in carvings dated to 3500 BCE.

CHAPTER THREE

Divine Royalty

THE GODS AND GODDESSES OF EGYPT

❧

IN THE valley of the two Niles, where the most fertile land sustains the peoples, the ancient Pharaohs traced their lineage back to the gods of Egypt. They were the first of the old civilisations to declare themselves not only blessed as rulers by the gods, but descended from gods themselves, and this allowed the Pharaohs to rule without question.

❧

The story goes that the very first ruler of Egypt was the great god Geb, god of the Earth, who was then succeeded by his son Osiris. When Osiris saw the people of Egypt he despaired of their barbarity and uncivilised ways and set about teaching them how to farm and store grain, how to live in peace with each other and create a society of art and science. He was aided in this by the god Thoth who helped give the Egyptian people writing and mathematics, as well as the goddess Ma'at who helped keep balance across all of life.

Much loved was Osiris by the people of Egypt, but his brother, Set, was jealous of Osiris's power and believed that it was he, not Osiris, who should have been given the kingdom.

Osiris's wife, Isis, caught Set plotting to take over the Land of the Nile and tried to warn her husband, but Osiris could not think badly of his beloved brother and did not heed Isis's warnings. Sure enough Set amassed an army of 72 soldiers who surprised Osiris in his throne room and murdered him, throwing his body into the Nile.

Set tried to coerce Isis into marrying him now that her husband was dead but instead Isis hurried to her sister Nephthys, a goddess charmed in the art of magic, and convinced her to perform a magic ritual to locate Osiris's remains. The spell worked and Isis rushed to the Nile to revive her husband with a special potion.

However, arriving at the river she encountered Set who had been lying in wait for her. He grabbed Osiris's body and tore it into fourteen pieces, which he scattered across the lands. Now surely Isis would realise her love was lost to her and become his.

But Isis's love for Osiris knew no bounds and for years she searched day and night across all the known lands until she found all fourteen pieces of her beloved. Her love for him was so great that just by the strength of her quest she was able to reassemble her dead husband and breathe life into him.

Yet he was too weak to go back to the kingdom and regain his rightful place. Isis and Osiris were only able to spend a few days together in each other's arms before Osiris passed into the land of the dead.

The sun rose in the east and Isis looked down on her dear one's face and knew that he had passed. She tearfully kissed him farewell and despite her grief she smiled, as she felt the stirring of their child within her. Their baby would be the true king of Egypt and remove any claim that Set had on the throne.

As Isis kissed her husband goodbye, Osiris left his mortal body and became the god of the afterlife, one of the most sacred gods in the Egyptian pantheon.

Isis stayed in Egypt and gave birth to their son, Horus, declaring him the true king of Egypt. Set refused to give up the throne but Isis was more beloved by the people and she had enough power to demand that the matter be settled by a jury of the gods. The trial lasted 40 years, during which time the child god grew into a man. After long deliberations Horus was declared the true and rightful king of Egypt.

Set was exiled from the kingdom, left to wander through the desert where he became the maker of sandstorms and desert droughts, wreaking his vengeance upon the people of Egypt whenever he could.

From that day forward all Pharaohs were said to descend from the line of Osiris and Isis, and claimed they alone would gain immortality and divinity after death.

﹋

The story of Isis and Osiris is a metaphor for resurrection and rebirth, a story which echoes the yearly flooding and withering of the Nile on which the Egyptian crops depended. This is why the river itself is featured so prominently in the story.

Despite the modern popularity of the Isis/Osiris creation myth, it is fairly recent in Egyptian terms, really only becoming popular during the last dynasty of the Egyptian Pharaohs. Before that time the Kings of Egypt did not consider themselves to be divine, but rather the representatives of the Egyptian Earth Mother and supreme goddess Ma'at. During these early dynasties Isis and Osiris were small, almost obscure deities who had few followers.

Rituals

Egyptian religion was highly ritualistic. The Pharaoh was the one true priest and was required to perform specific rituals at certain times of the year, particularly during the ever-important flooding of the Nile valleys. The Egyptian harvest of grain relied heavily on these yearly floods, which created the rich soil in which the seeds could be sown.

Rituals were highly organised around solar and lunar timings as well as annual celebrations and significant events, the most important being the death of a Pharaoh.

It is with the Egyptians that we see a clear political purpose for religion to create a ruling dynasty, a trend that was followed by the Abrahamic religions thousands of years later.

As the only representative of the gods and goddesses on the earthly plain, the Pharaoh was integral to the religious ceremonies that took place. This was not just a way to honour the gods but also helped strengthen the power and prestige of the Pharaohs themselves, so it was particularly important that all members of society took part or observed the festivals and ceremonies.

The Pharaoh's main ritual was the offering to Ma'at and Ra. Ma'at, the creator goddess was worshipped everywhere in Egypt and as such was arguably the most important and powerful deity in the Egyptian parthenon, even though there was no temple specifically dedicated to her.

Pharaohs would symbolically address Ma'at and Ra to gain insights and wisdom through complex and highly stylised rituals, often incorporating the slaughter of an animal such as a goat or ox and the readings of it entrails to gain divine prophesy of the year to come.

These rituals took place at the central shrine, dedicated to Ra, god of the Sun. Only the Pharaoh could open the locks on the door of this shrine, which were called the bolts of heaven, and the Pharaoh alone could enter the temple to 'see the face of the deity' and converse with the gods and goddesses.

He would then return from the temple to the awaiting crowd and relate to them the wisdom he had been offered by the grand deities.

Daily Rituals

The smaller temples allowed the common folk to come and maintain daily rituals called 'rehearsals of life', which usually entailed the faithful offering food or drink to a preferred god in return for a blessing.

The most popular deities were Ra, Ma'at, Nut and Geb; although specific requests could be more suited to specific gods. To ensure a good harvest one could make an offering to Hapi, the Egyptian river god. The goddess Sekhmet would be called upon to aid someone suffering from illness or to give comfort to those who were unwell.

Nocturnal Rituals

Death and the afterlife were important aspects of the Egyptian religions and night-time rituals were usually reserved for those requests which concerned death and funeral rites. These rituals were far more formal than the daily offering and required a priest anointed by the Pharaoh, or the Pharaoh himself, to oversee the ritual.

Only someone of status such as a relative of the Pharaoh would merit formal rites and monuments. However common folk could sleep overnight at a temple after making an offering. For this they would receive the gift of prophetic dreams, which could be interpreted by a priest at the temple, or a magi, for a small fee.

Festivals and Ceremonies

Most offerings and rituals were private affairs but, like the Sumerians before them, the Egyptian Pharaohs saw the benefits of grand large-scale events.

The annual flooding of the Nile and offering to the god Hapi, who oversaw this essential event, was celebrated with processions, galas and ceremonies leading up to and after the flood waters rose and receded.

There were other ceremonies, most of which were highly elaborate and dramatic performances of the great myths followed by massive offering of food and wine to the deities. In order to keep their popularity with the populace, later Pharaohs made sure that the ritualistic

offerings of food to the gods was symbolic and, after the
rites were performed, the food was redistributed to
the poor.

Death Rituals

The best known of all the Egyptian rituals are those
performed around the death of a Pharaoh. Any royal
funeral was a significant and ceremonial occasion, with
many months of preparation and the building of a funeral
monument called a pyramid.

When first envisaged by Ho-tep in the first dynasty of the Egyptian civilisation, the pyramids were reasonably simple structures but by the last dynasty these monuments were so elaborate they had to be started in the early years of the Pharaoh's reign and then held in readiness for their eventual death and rebirth into the afterlife.

Funeral ceremonies were extravagant affairs, with the bodies mummified using oils and spices. The important organs, such as heart and brain were removed from the bodies and encased in pottery jars, usually mummified or embalmed to ensure the Pharaoh could use them in their afterlife.

Anything seen as useful or important to the deceased was buried with them, including beloved servants (who were routinely massacred after the Pharaoh's death), valuable livestock, as well as weapons, jewellery and coins. Because of their treasures the burial sites were reportedly sealed with magical curses and filled with protective amulets.

Highly illustrative stories in hieroglyphics, a form of pictorial writing, were designed on the interior walls to remind the gods of the names and life stories of the deceased, to better safeguard their easy entry into the afterlife.

Important Egyptian Deities

There were thousands of different gods and goddesses worshipped throughout the two kingdoms of Egypt, with different deities becoming more prominent in later

dynasties. However it was the great Ennead, nine gods
and goddesses worshipped at the Heliopolis (Sun Temple)
which remain the best known entities today, and the royal
family of deities from which the Pharaohs claimed their
regal lineage.

The Nine Ennead

Name	Rules	Known for
Atum *Amun-Ra* *Amen* *Amen Ra* Supreme Entity of the Great Ennead	Fertility and creation later became the Sun god Ra	The consort of Ma'at. The Pharaoh and his wife would visit the Ra temple to get blessings for child bearing.
Geb *Keb* *Qeb* *Seb* God with the head of a snake, bull or ram	Earth	One of the few ancient male Earth gods, he is sometimes symbolised holding a goose, as he created the goose egg out of which the sun was hatched.
Isis	Motherhood, royalty, family commitment	A small regional fertility goddess fashioned after Ishtar who became a national Egyptian mother goddess.

Name	Rules	Known for
Nephthys	Magic, comfort and consolation	Goddess who comforts those who are in mourning. She presides over funerals and is a compassionate, loving figure.
Nut	The sky and the stars	Swallows the god Ra each night before birthing him again each day. Mothered Isis, Osiris, Set and Nephthys.
Osiris First Pharaoh	Rebirth, regeneration, afterlife	Nurturer of human kind and the god whose rebirth forms the basis of the royal lineage of the Pharaohs.
Set	Anarchy, storms, war and deserts	The most traditionally evil of the Egyptian gods, his rivalry with his brother Osiris may form the basis of the Biblical story Cain and Abel.
Shu	Original primordial god of air	Holds his daughter Nut in place to ensure the sky always remains stable.
Tefnut	Water	Mother of Nut and Geb, the goddess of moisture and wetness.

Name	Rules	Known for
OTHER IMPORTANT DEITIES		
Anubis Jackal-headed God	Guide of the dead	Guides and protects the dead. He is depicted as jackal-headed, as jackals were a common sight around graveyards, often scavenging and digging up remains.
Ammit Crocodile-headed demon goddess	Destruction devourer of souls	Fearsome goddess who emerges from the abyss to devour any soul found unworthy of the afterlife.
Bast *Alirus* *Bastet* *Ubaset* Cat or Lioness-headed goddess	Protection, fertility, long life and patron of cats	As she protected cats, Egyptians would often throw felines into inflamed buildings believing Bast would then extinguish the fires.
Hapi Hermaphrodite god sometimes given the head of a hippo	The River Nile, abundance	Hapi watches over the ebb and flow of the river Nile accompanied by a number of frog goddesses who sing to him and provide music for his joyful life.

Name	Rules	Known for
Hathor Cow-headed goddess	Love and happiness, music	Despite her beloved status, Hathor is credited with a massacre of the Nile people after they were heard drunkenly jeering at her beloved Ra.
Horus Falcon-headed son of Osiris and Isis	The sky and Sun, foresight	The eye of Horus is a potent protection talisman and is painted on seagoing vessels and worn as an amulet, even today.
Ma'at *Mut* Ancient goddess from the middle kingdoms	Divine Order, truth and justice	Ma'at weighs the human heart against a feather in the underworld to determine if one is worthy to enter the underworld.
Sekhmet Lion-headed goddess	Healing and medicine, war and vengeance	Loved as a powerful protector and healer, she is also said to be vengeful if wronged and is the destroyer of mankind in the holy writings.
Seshat Human-like goddess	Books, writing, libraries, astronomy, architecture and archives	Worshipped by architects and offerings are made to her during all the great building works, including the great pyramids.

Name	Rules	Known for
Thoth Ibis-headed god	Writing, logic, mathematics and intelligence	Thoth maintains balance and gives sage counsel to the other gods.
Wadjet Originally a local goddess of Buto	Protector of Pharaohs and women in childbirth	Wadjet provided a safe haven for the god Horus during his battle against Set.

Gods on Screen

Isis is perhaps the most well known of the Egyptian gods in modern popular culture, becoming somewhat of a feminist icon in later years. Versions of the goddess have appeared in a number of entertainment projects including a short-lived superhero television show of the 1980s called *The Secrets of Isis* which ran on American network CBS from 1975–1977. This show was the precursor to more popular female-superhero shows of the era, such as *Wonder Woman* and *The Bionic Woman* which debuted a few years after *Isis* was cancelled.

The Egyptian pantheon also turned up as the inspiration of the alien race in the original *Stargate* movie, although less so in the later television adaptation. Most recently the god Horus was the main subject of the multi-million-dollar sci-fi epic *Gods of Egypt* (2016) directed by Australian filmmaker Alex Proyas. This feature reimagined the ancient Egyptian gods as heroes in a modern action adventure film.

Egyptian exhibitions in museums and art galleries across the world continue to draw crowds and the design and graphic nature of the artworks and hieroglyphs have been a source of inspiration for artists and filmmakers for decades.

CHAPTER FOUR

Haven't I Seen You Somewhere Before?

THE GRECO- ROMAN PANTHEON

꧁꧂

ANCIENT GREECE is acknowledged as the birthplace of modern Western thought and it is from this civilisation that we have gained many of our modern concepts of philosophy, psychology, arts and science.

One might think that the gods and goddesses of such a civilisation would be rational, calm, collected and mature. That was certainly not the case with the deities of Olympus who governed over one of the most important phases of human endeavour.

The Greek gods and goddesses were dramatic, lively and the basis of some of the best stories in human history. Greek and later Roman writers delighted in retelling the salacious, tragic, sorrowful and immoral tales of these most human of gods.

They also proved to be incredibly resilient to invasion and erasure. When the Roman armies invaded Greece the Greek pantheon were so compelling they were instantly adopted by the Romans, who made virtually no changes to their mythology except giving most of them Latin names.

In modern times we know these deities as the Greco-Roman pantheon and we commemorate them in both their Greek and Roman versions throughout much of our modern Western culture.

Gods at War

The deities we usually associate with the Greco-Roman empire are the Olympians, headed by the god of lightning, Zeus and his sister wife, Hera. However these were not the original creator gods and goddesses of the universe in Greek mythology.

It was the Titans, more like primordial forces than human-like gods, who created the world from nothing and fashioned the universe, seas, forests and planets.

Unlike the Olympians, the Titans did not have a male-dominated power structure but a power-couple structure where the male and female entity would form together to create the forces of nature from which all creation emerged.

Clash of the Titans

Zeus, the son of the most powerful Titans of all, Cronus and Rhea, orchestrated the overthrow of the Titans.

Not all the old Titans were killed in this battle, and the survivors where exiled to Tartarus, a black abyss of despair and horror. The Titan children, Dione, Leto, Prometheus, Atlas and Epimetheus were spared this fate and all except Atlas allowed to be part of the new pantheon. Atlas was punished by Zeus for fighting against him in the Titan wars and forced to hold up the sky for all eternity. In later retellings, Atlas was said to be holding up the world itself.

Atlas's punishment was light compared to his cousin Prometheus's, who later invoked Zeus's wrath when he stole fire to give it to human beings.

Zeus tasked his cousins, Prometheus and Epimetheus to populate the Earth with all living creatures. Epimetheus fashioned the most beautiful and exotic animals, ensuring each had what they needed to survive in the world, including fur or feathers for warmth and teeth, tusks and claws for protection.

Prometheus was left to work on the last of the creatures, humankind. But his brother had left him no fur and feathers to cover the creatures' nakedness. There were no great teeth or talons, no wings or flippers. All Prometheus could give them to survive the harsh elements of the world was quick thinking.

Prometheus worried about these vulnerable pink things left in a world full of terrors, unprotected and vulnerable. So, one day he stole into the great palace of Zeus and, with the aid of Athena, took a torch of the eternal fire and brought it down to his shivering humans to provide them with light and warmth. The humans huddled in the glow of the fire and Prometheus was gladdened.

From Mount Olympus, Zeus saw the light on Earth and knew that the great fire had been stolen. Prometheus tried to reason with the king of the gods but the wrathful Zeus punished Prometheus for his theft by exiling him to a rocky mountainous outcrop where he was chained for eternity. Every day a giant eagle would descend on the bound Titan and rip out his innards. Being immortal, Prometheus would regenerate overnight only to be feasted upon the next day; day after day, tormented and tortured forever.

This story is just one example of how vengeful, cruel and uncaring the Greek gods could be and how little they truly cared for the beings they ruled over.

~~

Family Trees

In the Greek divine hierarchy, family connections formed the basis of the positions of power enjoyed by each of the gods and goddesses. Just like in Greek society itself, your lineage mattered and power was shared through documented family dynasties.

After the defeat of the Titans, the six children of Croneus and Rhea; Hera, Demeter, Hestia, Poseidon, Hades and Zeus, became the ruling family of the new Olympian pantheon. Demeter and Hestia soon removed themselves from the centre of power in Olympus and became hearth and harvest goddesses, living more closely with the people on Earth. The three brothers, Poseidon, god of the sea, Hades, god of the underworld and Zeus, god of the sky were originally equally powerful, but over time Zeus came to be supreme. This was partly due to his marriage to his sister Hera, which helped establish them as the power couple of Olympus.

·MIDAS' DAUGHTER·TURNED·TO·GOLD·

Zeus and Hera weren't the only incestuous union in the Greek divine realm. Hades abducted and married his niece Persephone, daughter of his sister Demeter.

Incest was a good way to cement the idea of family dynasty and help categorise all the different gods and goddesses through their familial connections to the key Olympians. Yet being the child of an incestuous Olympian union didn't necessarily guarantee power.

Hera and Zeus had a number of children, but only their son Ares gained any influence within the pantheon. Real power was wielded by Zeus's other children, which he had with a variety of goddesses, humans and nymphs.

One of the most important and powerful of Zeus's children was the goddess Athena, his child with the sea nymph, Metis. Athena became the patron goddess of Athens, the most powerful city state in Ancient Greece.

Zeus also fathered the sun god Apollo and his twin sister Artemis, goddess of the hunt with the Titan goddess Dione. He fathered Persephone with his sister Demeter and the Muses with the Titan goddess Mnemosyne – translated in modern language as memory. He also fathered Aphrodite, the goddess of love and Hermes, messenger of the gods.

Zeus also chased after human women, some of which bore him children. Dionysus, god of wine and grapes was actually half-human and the only human-born child to be considered a fully fledged Olympic god. Zeus's other two half human children were the famous hero Heracles and the hermaphrodite child Agetis.

Despite his adultery, Hera stayed loyal to Zeus. She saved her worst punishments for his bastard children or the women who drew Zeus's affections, even though often such affections were unwanted and unrequited.

Gifts From the Gods

Despite their pettiness, jealousy, lust and downright criminal behaviour, the gods and goddesses of Olympus were also quite willing and able to bestow great gifts upon their human followers, if it amused them to do so. They would intervene in wars and often descend onto the earthly plans and interact with their human creations.

Whenever a god gave a mortal a gift, however, it was wise for the recipient to think twice before accepting it. Often these gifts came with a great, unexpected cost which could end up causing nothing but chaos and heartbreak.

King Midas, one of the most famous mortal figures in Greek mythology, was offered a gift of his choice from the god Dionysus, who appreciated the king's protection of his beloved satyr Selil. Midas immediately asked that Dionysus grant him the ability to turn everything he touched to gold. Dionysus at first hesitated but Midas insisted that this was his greatest wish, and Dionysus eventually granted the request.

At first this seemed to answer all of Midas's dreams but soon the true nature of the gift became apparent. Midas, upon taking the hand of his beloved daughter, turned her into a golden statue. He was unable to eat or drink anything, for all that came near his lips or hands was transmuted into inedible gold. The king became isolated and mad before he eventually died of starvation.

The story of King Midas is not just a mortality tale about greed but also about the issues with human free will and poor decision-making.

Rituals and Ceremonies

Celebrations and ceremonies for the Gods were usually scheduled around a series of holy days throughout the year, each dedicated to one of the major deities. However, many gods also had devoted followers who formed cults of worship, including a dedication ceremony of themselves as sacred servants of the temple and offerings of food and wine.

Giving up of luxuries and self-sacrifice was a common offering to the gods from devotees. The famous Vestal Virgins promised to remain chaste and refused marriage and child rearing as a measure of their devotion to the goddess Vesta (the Roman version of Hestia). It is probably from this practice that the tradition of celibacy came to be incorporated into the Latin Catholic church in later centuries, although men, as well as women, made this oath as Catholic priests and nuns.

Prophesy and Oracles

The ancient Greeks, and later the Romans, had a strong belief in the power of oracles and seers to give them glimpses into the future and form a direct line to their Gods. Greek priests read the entrails of animals to determine messages from the gods and often used their interpretations of these to instruct kings and lords on important military matters.

The most famous oracle was said to be the Oracle of Delphi, dedicated to the god Apollo. Pilgrims could journey to the site, which was marked with a deep dark well, and once there would ask their questions. Answers would often be related to them in prophetic dreams, which they would go to a seer or priest to interpret.

Several of the great stories in the Greco-Roman myths relate to seers giving grave and potent predictions to kings, gods and heroes.

Important Greco-Roman Deities

Name (Roman and Greek)	Rules over	
THE TITANS		
Greek Chaos and Nyx – Greek and Roman	Original creator god and goddess	The idea that all life comes from Chaos is based on the myth of Nyx (nothing) and Chaos coming together and creating the universe.
Coeus and Phoebe – Greek and Roman	Titan creators of the moon	Father and mother of Leto who birthed Artemis and Apollo.
Croneus and Rhea – Greek **Saturn and Cybele** – Roman	King and queen of the Titans and the co-creators of harvests and plenty	Croneus is now commemorated as Father Time. It is from his name that we get the modern words 'chronology' and 'chronicles'.
Dione – Greek and Roman	None	Zeus's first wife, she was mother of the goddess Aphrodite.

Name (Roman and Greek)	Rules over	
Eros – Greek **Cupid** – Roman	Titan god of love and desire	The saying 'love is blind', comes from the story of Eros and his lover Pysche who broke her promise never to look upon his face. When she did, he left never to return.
Gaia – Greek **Maia** – Roman	Earth goddess	Earth Mother worshipped as the creator of all life. In modern culture – Mother Nature.
Hyperion and Theia – Greek and Roman	Titan god and goddess of the Sun	Parents of Selene (Moon) Helios (Sun) and Eos (Dawn).
Iapetus and Theia – Greek and Roman	Titan god and goddess of the planets, justice	Parents of the forgotten Olympians: Prometheus, Atlas and Epimetheus.
Mnemosyne and Crius – Greek and Roman	Titan god and goddess of memory and nostalgia	From her name we get the word 'memory', the most powerful inspiration. She was mother to the nine muses.
Oceanus and Tethys – Greek and Roman	Father and mother of all the oceanids and the creator of all the rivers and waterways	Parents of Dione.

Name (Roman and Greek)	Rules over	
THE OLYMPIANS		
Aphrodite – Greek **Venus** – Roman	Goddess of love and beauty	Famed for her beauty and her famous magical girdle that made her irresistible to all.
Apollo – Greek and Roman	God of arts, music and sometimes conflated with Helios as the god of the Sun	One of the most loved of the Greek gods and the only one to keep his name during the assimilation into Roman mythology.
Ares – Greek **Mars** – Roman	War	One of the few of Hera's children with Zeus to gain a place in the ruling Olympian pantheon.
Artemis – Greek **Diana** – Roman	Goddess of the hunt and the forests Twin sister of Apollo	Strong and independent, she once caught a hunter spying on her and transformed him into a stag, which her hunting dogs ran down and tore to pieces.
Athena – Greek **Minerva** – Roman	Goddess of wisdom, truth, war and patron of Athens	Born from a crack in Zeus's head after he swallowed her pregnant mother Metis.

Name (Roman and Greek)	Rules over	
Atlas – Greek and Roman	Holder of the heavens	Zeus punished Atlas for fighting against him by cursing him to forever hold up the great vaults of the sky.
Demeter – Greek **Ceres** – Roman	Goddess of the harvest, fields and grains	Her daughter's abduction by Hades is said to be the reason for the four seasons.
Dionysus – Greek **Bacchus** – Roman	God of wine, grapes and drunkenness	In Rome the annual festival, Bacchanalia is still commemorated in his honour.
Epimetus – Greek and Roman	Creator of animals and living things	His name means 'afterthought' as he did not leave enough creation material to adequately make human beings.
Hades – Greek **Pluto** – Roman	God of the underworld	Hades is the name of both the god and the land in which he rules, an underworld which is both a place of punishment and reward.

Name (Roman and Greek)	Rules over	
Hephaestus – Greek **Vulcan** – Roman	God of fire and blacksmiths	Born a cripple, Hephaestus was thrown from a mountain by his mother Hera. He survived the fall and later was married to the goddess Aphrodite.
Hera – Greek **Juno** – Roman	Queen of the gods, rules over marriage, childbirth and protector of women	Married to Zeus; sister of Hades, Zeus, Demeter, Poseidon. Mother to Hephaestus, Ares and Discordia. A powerful and vengeful goddess.
Poseidon – Greek **Neptune** – Roman	God of the sea	One of the mightiest gods to the seafaring Greeks.
Prometheus – Greek and Roman	Creator of Mankind	Prometheus created human beings and stole fire from Zeus to warm them.
Zeus – Greek **Jupiter** – Roman	King of the gods and rules the sky, thunder and lightning	Husband and brother to Hera, brother to Hades, Demeter and Poseidon. Father to many gods, goddesses and demigods.

Gods with Feet of Clay

The Greek gods had great power and required offerings and rituals to retain their favour – but they were not infallible nor particularly wise. They were in fact often petty, jealous, immoral, careless and downright inattentive towards their subjects. They could, and did, make mistakes, acted on whim rather than reason and could be emotional creatures. But rather than making them less beloved, this endeared them more to their people, who felt their gods were approachable, malleable and potentially bested.

These gods could be seduced, enticed, moved and angered by their followers in ways that weren't seen in religions past. For the first time the relationship with the gods was not such an unequal one, with all the power in the hands of the immortals.

This was incredibly important because if their gods didn't know all the answers then humans could try to solve some of their own. Human invention and creativity, thought and philosophy could thrive under these gods in ways that absolute divinities would never allow.

The gods of the Greek pantheon would agree they were flawed – but they were by far the best gods to influence such a period of thought and scientific evolution.

CHAPTER FIVE

Gods in a Rational World

THE GODS AND GODDESSES OF ANCIENT CHINA

❦

WHILE THE human-like gods and goddesses of Europe were squabbling, blessing and provoking their worshippers, a very different type of deity was being created across the Far East.

The deities of the Asian continent, spanning Mongolia and China, across to the islands of Japan, down into the subcontinent and across the southeast were based upon two opposing and yet complementary ideologies: animism, the idea that the land itself was a spiritual force; and the philosophy of rationalism, that by understanding the cycles of nature and themselves, any person could reach god-like status through the development of rational thought, reflection and enlightened thinking.

In the ancient kingdoms of China the rational gods of Taoism, Buddhism and Confucianism sat alongside ancient animist gods and goddesses, monsters, demons and mythical creatures.

The playfulness and unpredictability of these divine creatures give the myths of China a host of cheeky, irrepressible characters, as well as a very complex morality with social lessons that crossed language and cultural barriers.

Taoism, Confucianism and Buddhism

One of the earliest religions of China was that of Taoism, still practised today in some areas of China and Japan. The philosophy of Tao, translated roughly as 'the way', focuses on the idea of living in harmony with the natural world. The Tao, or Dao, which is a more literal phonetic translation of the original word, was a rather mysterious force. A creator energy, which unified the world and kept order.

It was not personified as a physical entity and as such it became more of a general principle upon which the other gods and goddesses could judge their behaviour and therefore became very accommodating to a host of different regional divinities.

As with most Ancient asian belief systems, the Tao was as much a philosophical ideology as a religious practice and believers would engage in rites and rituals such as meditation,

Feng Shui and fortune telling as well as the reading and chanting of scriptures – called the Tao Te Ching.

In China, most of those we would now consider ancient Chinese gods were in fact appropriated from other regions and assimilated into the ideals of Taoism which then spread back across Asia to be re-adopted by the worshippers of the original deity. It was a very efficient and effective system of religious transference.

Tao itself is not technically a god, although Taoists do refer to Tao in a god-like language and sometimes refer to the revered founder of Taoism, Lao Tsu as a god and the personification of Tao. He was however a mortal and at least in the first telling of the works, a philosopher and wise man, not a heavenly all-knowing god.

Buddhism and the Tao

The Chinese Tao influence on Buddhism cemented many of the traditions we now associate with the Enlightened One. Like Lao Tzu, it is believed that Buddha was originally a mortal man, a prince of India called Siddhartha who, upon seeing the emptiness of his luxurious existence, sat under the sacred Bodhi tree until he found enlightenment.

Enlightenment, in the Buddhist tradition, is great inner knowledge and ascension of self into a godhead, but it was quite accommodating to the immortality ideals of Taoism. The Buddha is seen as gaining immortality through the transcendence of human consciousness and so becomes a spiritual being. His mortal beginning is seen as evidence that any human has the potential to also gain this most sacred of mental states and become a Buddha themselves.

Confucius Says...

Confucianism was the next great religion to dominate greater China. This belief system became popular during a period of civil and political unrest of the Han Dynasty of 220–206 BCE.

Like Tao and Buddhism, Confucianism was linked to teachings of a great teacher and philosopher Kongzi, who lived between 551 and 479 BCE. Later philosophies of the teachers Mencius (339 BCE) and Xunzi (256 BCE), were also incorporated into the teachings of Confucianism and attributed to one idealised teacher now named Confucius.

Confucianism, or Ru-Jai doctrine as it is known in China, is a thoroughly humanist and rational approach to the great questions of life. It focuses on looking at everyday concerns rather than trying to solve large existentialist questions about the meaning of life.

Confucianism is probably the most psychological of the Asian belief systems, consistently drawing the spiritual conversation into the personal. In Confucianism, the practice of worshipping a spirit is impossible until one understands oneself and the functions of everyday existence.

Chinese Folk Beliefs and the Old Gods

The Buddha, Confucius and The Tao are states of being, which can be achieved by those who commit themselves to the practices of thought; including care of nature, self-purification, vegetarianism, meditation, reflection, humanism, and consciousness. As such their worship allowed many regional gods and goddesses to be kept and incorporated into the belief systems across China and South East Asia. In many cases the old gods and goddesses stories were rewritten to include encounters with the Buddha or the Tao.

One of the most important aspects of ancient Chinese religion were the nine great goddesses who watched over mothers and children, originally believed to come from the Chinese folk beliefs of the peoples of northern China.

Lead by the supreme mother of the heavens Bixia, the nine goddesses each had a particular area of interest and concern. There was Bānzhěn Niángniáng a goddess who protected children, Cuīshēng Niángniáng who looked after easy births and protected midwives and Nǎimǔ Niángniáng whose sole focus was ensuring maternal milk was safe and protected.

The goddess Péigū Niángniáng watched over young girls, while Zǐsūn Niángniáng watched over offspring more generally. There was a specific goddess, Yǎnguāng Niángniáng who protected eyesight, as without a careful

eye children could go missing, and the final of the nine goddesses, Péiyǎng Niángniáng, was said to guide young children in education and moral virtues.

Goddess worship was extremely common across China with the altars usually arranged with Bixia centrally located flanked by whichever of the goddesses were needed in the household.

Other goddesses included the Silkworm Maiden, the goddess of the Three Isles and the best named of any domestic goddess, the goddess who sweeps clean, Sǎoqīng Niángniáng.

Mother of Compassion

Another ancient Asian goddess who was easily incorporated into the teachings of Buddhism was the goddess of mercy, Quan Yin who was worshipped across Asia, particularly in Vietnam, Japan, Indonesia, India and China.

Quan Yin was known to comfort anyone who cried out in suffering and her unconditional love was seen as a facet of the enlightenment that could be offered by the teachings of the Buddha.

There are many varied origin stories for Quan Yin, which is not surprising considering how many countries call her their own. In the Taoist tradition she is born from the rainbow to bring comfort, and stop the tears of the heavens (rain) with a message of love and hope.

Her more common legend is more traditionally Buddhist in origin. In this version Quan Yin was a mortal girl, daughter of an Indian prince, who, like the Buddha, rejected the trappings of wealth and determined to live a life of self-sacrifice and service to others. She attained Buddhahood through her compassion and selfless love, but refused to transcend from the humans she cared for and instead became an immortal goddess who protected the people, particularly women.

Later the legend was changed to give Quan Yin Chinese heritage and she was transformed into the princess Guanyin, Daughter of the Chou dynasty. In this version Guanyin wanted to become a nun but her regal father would not allow it and punished her harshly for refusing to marry the man of his choice. He ordered that she perform menial tasks for the poor and ill, but Guanyin loved these people and showed them great kindness. Enraged that this humiliation had not worked on his daughter and that she still disobeyed him, the Emperor ordered that she was to be executed by sword in the public courtyard.

The executioner however, was softened by the loveliness and kindness of Guanyin's nature and beauty, and instead of running her through, broke the sword into forty thousand pieces.

Her father, still intent on his punishment, had her suffocated and sent to hell for disobedience. According to this story Guanyin descended to Hell but once there she turned the flames to blossoms and the austere bleak plains into meadows and waterfalls to quench the thirst of the damned. Yama, the god of the afterworld gave her immortality and sent her back to the mortal world. She ascended on a lotus flower.

When she returned to the palace she found her father was gravely ill. In her compassion Guanyin cut her own flesh to make medicine and cured him.

Overcome by her forgiveness and self-sacrifice, he declared his daughter a divine lady and ordered that statues praising her divinity were carved throughout the land.

The story of Quan Yin/ Guanyin, whichever one is seen as true or more useful, serves as a beautiful allegory about the power of love and forgiveness to achieve enlightenment and immortality.

Important Ancient Chinese Deities

Name	Rules	Myths
Baidi White deity, Great deity of the Western Peak Origin: Chinese folk religion	Metal and autumn	He is the white dragon of the Sìhǎi Lóngwáng.
Běiyuèdàdì Black deity, Great deity of the Northern Peak Origin: Chinese folk religion	War, water and winter	A dark warrior or a black dragon.

Name	Rules	Myths
Bixia Lady of the blue dawn, Heavenly immortal lady, Holy Mother of nine skies, Lady of Mount Tai Origin: Northwest China	Mother goddess of the heavens and ruling goddess of the nine great goddesses of the Chinese pantheon	Most important of the nine great Chinese goddesses. Identified by Tao worshippers as the ancient goddess of Northwest China.
Cashien Origin: Chinese folk religion	Wealth god	Can bestow wealth on any who cross paths with him.
Douma Mother of meaning Origin: Chinese folk religions	Creation and protector goddess	Douma is represented by the Big Dipper star system.
Quan Yin/ Guanyin She who hears the cries of the world Origin: India	Goddess of compassion and mercy	Female personification usually shown riding a lotus, crying tears of compassion or holding an infant.

Name	Rules	Myths
Liuxian Immortal Liu Origin: Northwest Chinese folk religions	Immortal snake god from the zoomorphic gods of Northwest China	Usually represented as a large python or viper.
Nine goddesses of motherhood Origin: Northwest China	Protectors of mothers and children	Worshipped throughout the stages of child-rearing.
Pa-hsien The Eight Immortals Origin: Taoism	Immortality	Thought to be the original eight scholars of the Han Dynasty, they achieved immortality by eating the sacred peach.
Pangu Origin: Chinese folk religion	Yin and Yang	Pangu separated the earth and the heavens and created the idea of balance – yin and yang.
Sanhuang The three patrons Origin: Chinese folk religions	Fuxi – heaven Nuwa – Earth Shennong – humankind	Fuxi is seen as a divine emperor, Nuwa as a graceful woman and Shennong appears as a lowly peasant or the red dragon.

Name	Rules	Myths
Sìhǎi Lóngwáng Dragon kings of the four seas Origin: Southwest China	The seas and the four cardinal compass points	The four great dragons of creation, work alongside Tian, the yellow dragon at the centre of the universe.
Sun Wukong Monkey King Origin: India	Warrior God	Original Tao/animist deity. His story is an allegory of the struggle between the Buddhists and the Tao.
Tàihào Great deity of the Eastern Peak, Green or Blue-green deity Origin: Chinese folk religion	Fertility and spring	Usually represented by the blue/green dragon and is the consort of the goddess Bixia.
Tian, Highest deity, deity, being that gives birth to all things Also known as: *Shangdi Tiānshén Tian, Yudi* Origin: Various deities across South and North China	Primordial creation god; it is represented as a continuing heavenly force in many guises	Tian is the supreme force in the universe from which all things are created. Sometimes represented as a yellow dragon.

Name	Rules	Myths
Xiwangmu Queen Mother of the West Origin: Northwest China	Inspiration, death and immortality	She is considered as both a terrifying and benign goddess who is symbolised by weaving and the totem of the tiger.
Yanwang Purgatory King Origin: Chinese folk religion, Taoist practice	Ruler of the underworld	Often portrayed as the manifestation of yin and yang principles in Tao religion.
Yuexia Laoren Old man of the Moon Origin: Chinese folk religion	Matchmaker, patron of true love	The Moon is seen as an elixir for lovers.

The Monkey God

Sun Wukong, the monkey god was a cheeky, playful and chaotic immortal who was born from a stone and became the monkey king. Sun Wukong was an extremely strong, agile and skilled warrior with supernatural powers, including the ability to turn each one of his monkey hairs into clones of himself to help him win impossible battles.

Sun Wukong was originally a Taoist idea born from chaos, but was later incorporated into the Buddhist tradition through the Chinese mythological story *\ Journey to the West*. In this story Sun Wukong is tasked by a Buddhist monk, to help him retrieve the original Buddhist writings from India and bring them to the Chinese emperor. The monk and the monkey king are aided on this quest by several Chinese gods and goddesses, monsters and spirits as well as the Buddha.

The *Journey to the West* was reimagined for modern audiences as the Japanese-produced television show *Monkey*, which was made between 1978–1980 and viewed across the world in dubbed versions in English and other languages.

The Gods Under Communist Rule

After the 1949 Communist uprising in China all religions were put under strict governmental control. Over the next few years religious intolerance grew and during the 1966 Cultural Revolution under Mao Zedong all religious worship was outlawed. Anyone found engaging in religious practices could be imprisoned for up to thirty years.

Quan Yin – Goddess of Compassion

After Mao's death in 1976 the ban on religions started to ease and now the Chinese Communist government recognises five official Chinese religions including Tao, Buddhism, Islam, Catholicism and Protestant Christianity. However the gods and goddesses of the traditional Chinese folk beliefs are still unwelcome and the deities of old now exist mainly in exile through the animistic beliefs of tribespeople in Nepal, Tibet, India, Bali and Mongolia.

Gods by Numbers

Numbers play an important part in the lives of the divinities. In Greek mythology the number three was particularly common — the Three Fates, the Nine Muses (divisible by three) and the Three Graces, to name but a few. Three is also incorporated into the aspects of the triple goddess in Celtic mythology (mother/maiden/crone), and the holy trinity in modern Christianity.

In Chinese mythology the numbers **four**, representative of the four cardinal directions, **eight**, representing infinity and **nine**, indicating completion, were used to create connections and philosophical meanings for the divinities. Numerology was then used in fortune telling, Feng Shui and Chinese astrology, all spiritual rituals and practices under the Tao and Buddhist traditions.

Chinese Mythology and Popular Culture

Despite the fact that China has been somewhat isolated culturally during its communist years, there have been many representations of Chinese mythology in Asian and Western popular culture.

Martial arts films coming out of Hong Kong have included fantasy storylines which use ancient Chinese deities, and the Chinese film industry has started taking up this trend through the release of some major co-productions with mythological aspects.

Kung Fu Hustle (2015) and *Detective Dee and the Mysterious Flame* are two recent Chinese films which used deities from the old Chinese folk tales to tell fun, adventurous stories. Both are readily available and have done well at the Chinese and international box office.

Western writers and filmmakers have also borrowed elements from Chinese mythology. In the German children's book, *The Never-Ending Story* by Michael Ende, the luck dragon Falor is based on Baidi, the white dragon of Chinese myth.

However, the real impact of Chinese mythology has been in the areas of alternative health and healing where Taoist and Buddhist practices such as Feng Shui, Tai Chi, Reflexology and meditation have been taken up across the world as complementary and alternative health practices.

CHAPTER SIX

The Warriors in the Sky

THE NORSE GODS AND GODDESSES

❧

IN THE great halls of Asgard the king of the Norse gods, Odin, sat at the head of the long table and watched as the other gods and goddesses feasted, laughed and enjoyed the evening. But Odin was troubled.

His wife Frigg, always attuned to her husband's moods, glanced at him with concern. He smiled at her, trying to reassure her, but she knew something was wrong and took his hand.

'What troubles you, husband?'

Odin lowered his head and looked down at his plate of meat, untouched, the fat solidified into a white glutinous mass. 'I saw the Volva today.'

Frigg shook her head. Nothing that woman told her husband ever bode well. The seer seemed to see only death and destruction. Usually Odin shook it off, they were warriors, well acquainted with bloodshed and horror, yet Frigg felt this time the Volva's prediction was more than the usual warning about the Ice Giants invading, or Loki creating turmoil in Valhalla.

'What did the old witch say?' Frigg asked, swallowing down the sense of dread she felt just asking the question.

Odin gazed with his one eye across the Ragna, or ruling family, who both loved and feared their king. These gods and goddesses of the North were fearless and strong, but they were not immortal. Like the humans they guided to the warriors' afterworld of Valhalla, the Norse deities could be killed, their long life created not by divinity but the charmed apples of Idun's garden.

Frigg followed her husband's gaze. Thor, his impossibly heavy hammer lying innocently on the table beside him, was tearing into a leg of pork while shouting across at the infernal god Loki to stop dancing on the table. Loki of course would not stop. Anything he could do to annoy the god of lightning gave him immeasurable pleasure.

Freya goddess of the sky, and the most powerful deity besides Odin himself, sat quietly in the corner, her amber necklace glowing softly around her beautiful neck. Tyr, Nott and Magni tried to gain Loki's attention reminding him they were in the midst of a fiercely competitive game of dice. The other gods also beseeched Loki to stop his shenanigans and get back to the game, as many of them had placed bets on the outcome. Unsurprisingly the most favoured to win was Loki, as everyone knew he would probably cheat and win the game.

'The day is coming, my love, when we will all be gone. Twilight approaches and there is nothing I can do about it,' Odin said quietly. Frigg turned to her husband again with alarm.

'When?'

Odin shook his head, 'I do not know. The Volva would say only that there will soon be a day when three roosters will crow and a hound deep in the bowels

Thor

of the earth will howl. At this time Sutr will rouse and come to us, with a sword brighter than the sun.'

'The fire giant? But surely he would lose against all the power of Asgard?'

Odin shook his head, 'I shall be devoured by Fenir the great wolf, son of Loki; who will betray us all. Thor defeated by Loki's other son, a mighty serpent, and only Freyr will be left to fight the giant. The Sun will become black and the Earth will drown in a great sea. The stars that watch over us will vanish and the blackness will engulf us all.'

Frigg looked at Odin in horror. 'But surely we must be able to prevent this! Rouse the gods. Destroy Sutr before he awakens.'

Odin patted Frigg's hand gently and looked at her through a tear-filled eye.

'The time of Asgard is passing, but the Volva says that another great hall will arise and those who we have lost will be returned to the world.'

Frigg's throat closed in as she thought of her beloved son, Baldr, the god of beauty and innocence, who was killed by his brother Hodor. Frigg never forgave her younger son for taking the fairest and best of her children from her, although she was fairly sure that the cowardly hand of Loki was somehow behind it.

'Baldr will be returned?'

Odin nodded his head, 'so she said'. He knew Baldur's death was Frigg's great sorrow, yet she would experience

many more before her beloved son would be released from the afterlife.

'Should we tell them?' Frigg asked, gesturing towards the hall full of deities. Odin shook his head. 'Why spoil their fun when nothing can be done for it? This is a secret for us to keep.'

Frigg nodded, her husband was wise in all things and she would follow his lead on this. Nevertheless she knew neither of them would sleep another night, their waking hours full with this knowledge.

✌

The Mortal Gods and the Legend of Ragnarok

The great deities of the Norse Germanic religions, worshipped by Vikings and Germanic tribes across Scandinavia, Germany and Iceland were a rowdy, loyal and courageous group who ruled over the clans of Europe with an iron-like fist.

Only warriors and those who died in battle could count on the Ragna, or Norse ruling gods to look out for them, and as a result the mythology of these gods revolved around war, trickery, death and destruction.

The most important myth of the Norse world was that of Ragnarok, a prophesy given to the ruling god Odin which foretold the end of the gods and the rise of a new world.

Described in length in the epic poem, *Edda*, written sometime prior to 10 AD, the myth of Ragnarok is not an account of an actual divine battle but rather a glimpse into the future for the gods themselves. The Ragnarok is similar to the Biblical prophecy of the Rapture where the world will be swept clean and a lost god (Jesus/Baldr) will be returned from death to rule the earth.

The legend of Ragnarok (roughly translated as the 'Doom of the Gods' or 'Twilight of the Gods') also reflected some of the elements of the epic Sumer poem, *Gilgamesh* although not specifically called a flood, the end of the world was prophesied as the sea swallowing the Earth.

The Volva who prophesied the Ragnarok is vague about the cause or reason for the flooding of the world, but she does state that the Earth will emerge from the sea and describes an eagle landing on a mountain and the surviving gods, which included the great goddesses, meeting together in a field to play a game of chance which brings back the harvests. Baldur and his brother Hodor are also brought back from the land of Helheim (the Norse afterworld where those not killed in battle must spend their days).

The fact of this prophesy and that the gods of Asgard were not immortal meant that they were one of the few divine realms who lived their lives under the shadow of death. Their focus on a good and honourable demise, usually achieved in battle, makes sense for gods who were aware of their own mortality.

The Importance of the Goddess

Norse goddesses were equally powerful as the male deities and in the prophesy of Ragnarok it is mainly the female deities who survive and go on to rule over a more peaceful land.

Goddesses were linked with the Volva Sedir or female witches and soothsayers of Viking and Germanic societies who, much like the medicine women of Africa and the Americas and the herbalists and witches of The British Isles, were held in high regard until the attack on female power by the Christian church.

Female goddesses Freya, Frigg and Idun watched over creation, life and death, similar to the three fates of

The prophesied battle of Ragnarok

Greco-Roman religions. Freya, the most powerful of the goddesses was seen as a powerful user of magic as well as the goddess of love and desire.

Enchanted objects are important aspects of the great goddesses and warrior women of mythology. Freya's necklace and Aphrodite's girdle both granted their goddesses the power of irresistibility. The Amazonian belts of strength and truth linked the female deities and warriors with jewellery and fashion accessories from the very first myths.

In the 1960s these items were reimagined into the DC comic character Wonder Woman, who incorporated the ancient goddesses' attributes of strength, justice and beauty. The character is named Diana after the Roman goddess of the hunt and she is characterised as an Amazonian princess assisted by the Ancient Greco-Roman gods. She is defined by her sexy outfit but also by her important accessories, a belt or girdle which gives her strength and heightened abilities and a golden lasso which insures anyone roped within it must tell the truth.

Goddess Freya meets the Dwarves

Rituals

Norse religion was worshipped throughout Germanica, Scandinavia and the British Isles, and for a time reached down into, and influenced Gaul.

It is seen as a folk or pagan religion, which means there were no specific organised churches that oversaw the rituals or worship but rather a communal faith which focused on village and small societal connections. There were some national festivals based around seasonal rites such as spring and harvest.

The Scandinavian and Germanic people did not create any written documentation around their actual rituals, and the myths and legends of their gods, although fairly well documented in epic forms of literature and poetry, are unclear in their connection to everyday common practices.

The pre-Christian European religions had no specific word for religion or organised worship although the word *Sidr*, meaning 'custom', was used to describe certain rituals, which could vary across geographical regions. Despite the huge distances between different geographical groups, the people knew and borrowed each other's customs, myths and practices leading to a fairly strong similarity across the different sacred ideas.

What little is known does suggest that sacrifice was a common element to most rituals and would usually entail the killing and then communal eating of a sacrificed animal, accompanied by the drinking of mead, a medieval form of honey wine. Feasting was done around specific calendar events and grains and ale were offered to the gods in exchange for fertility and good harvests.

Most of the documented information around Norse practices was completed by the Christian monks who saw the pagan religions as devil worshipping and so the tales of ritual and celebration are often conflated with ideas of witchcraft, satanic practices and evil.

The Norse goddess Hel was lost as a goddess and instead her name was used for the land of torment presided over by the male devil deity in Christian mythology. This effectively erased a powerful goddess and recast her as a symbol of damnation and torture.

The Viking Easter

Easter, celebrated today as a Christian festival to mark the death and resurrection of Christ, is actually based on the spring festivities for the Viking goddess Eostre for whom it is named.

Eostre is similar to the Sumerian goddess Ishtar who was also a spring deity who had the hare as her symbolic animal.

It is because of these two goddesses that we celebrate Easter with bunnies and eggs representing fertility and why this 'Christian' festival is celebrated at different dates each year, linking to the phases of the moon, sacred to the goddess.

Important Norse Deities

The deities and creatures of Norse legend consist of the gods of Asgard as well as the race of giants, elves, fairies and dwarves, many of whom were adopted into Germanic and Britannic folklore.

Name	Rules	
Baldur	God of beauty, innocence peace and rebirth	Baldur was the only Norse god to have near immortality. Mistletoe was the only thing which could harm him.
Bragi	Poetry, music and the harp	Bragi is destined to die in the battle of Ragnarok.
Eostre	Goddess of spring	Adopted by the Britannic tribes. The Christian festival of Easter is named after her.

Name	Rules	
Freya	Goddess of love, childbirth, crops, fertility, magic and compassion	Freya's key role is as collector of dead warriors and bringer of the Northern Lights.
Freyr Twin brother of Freya	God of fertility and prosperity, Patron-god of Sweden	Has a magical sword that can fight by itself. He is killed with this very sword in Ragnarok.
Frigg Wife of Odin	Marriage, motherhood, managing the household, prophesy	Frigg foresaw the death of her beloved son Baldur but was unable to save him.
Hel	Goddess of the Helheim, the underworld for those who do not die in battle.	After Ragnarok, Hel will ascend from the afterworld and be one of the great rulers of the new realms.
Hermod *Hermodr*	Heroes and bravery	Hermod vainly tried to save Baldur after he was fatality injured.
Hodor *Hodr*	God of winter	Blind god tricked by Loki into killing his brother Baldur with a mistletoe-tipped spear.

Name	Rules	
Idun *Iounn*	Goddess of youth, guardian of sacred apples	Loki once stole Idun and gave her to the giant eagle Thjazi. The gods made Loki rescue the goddess and return her to the garden.
Joro	Goddess of the Earth	Mother of Thor, she is said to survive Ragnarok.
Loki	Trickster and god of mischief	Not the son of Odin but the child of the giant Farbauti and Laufey, whose status is unclear but could be a goddess.
Nanna	Goddess of joy and peace	Beloved minor goddess.
Odin *Woden* *Wode*	King of the gods, ruler of Asgard	The most powerful warrior of Asgard, Odin lost an eye in the fight against the ice giants, the god's mortal enemy.
Oor	No specific ruling	Oor is a somewhat mysterious god mentioned only in relation to his wife Freya.
Tyr	God of war and the skies	A hearty and well-loved god in a culture which enjoyed fighting.

Name	Rules	
Thor	God of lightning	Symbolised by his hammer which is so heavy no other deity can lift it. An honourable god who helps out others, particularly Freya.
Vali	Vengeance	He slew the god Hodor and blinded Loki in retaliation for their involvement in the death of Baldur.

The Influence of Norse Religion

Norse religion had a huge effect upon the spiritual beliefs across Europe. Although somewhat influenced itself by the Greco-Roman gods and goddesses, Norse deities were more metaphorical than literal and this allowed them to spread across Europe and meld with the Celtic and Roman divinities.

Many of the characters and stories of the Norse myths form the basis of modern fantasy books such as *Lord of the Rings* by JRR Tolkien and *Songs of Ice and Fire* – the books upon which the popular television *Game of Thrones* is based, written by George RR Martin. Elves, dwarves, giants and trolls all originally appeared in Norse mythology before being adopted into the fairy realm and fantasy fiction.

The Norse goddesses, erased from more modern religious iconography appear as the queens, witches and princesses of many of our modern fairytales.

The story of 'Snow White and the Seven Dwarves' is a retelling of the goddess Freya's encounter with a group of ugly dwarves who enticed her to lie with them in exchange for a necklace which granted her the gift of irresistibility.

The modern version has been sanitised but the key elements of the original myth, the dwarf characters, the beautiful young woman feared for her power and the connections, still recognisable. Other elements of Norse and Celtic mythology were also injected into the tale, particularly the characterisation of the wicked queen, a demonised version of the goddess Frigg, who was herself a stepmother to many of the Norse gods and was known in the Norse religion to have the gift of prophesy which was represented in the folk/fairy tale by the talking mirror.

The use of the poisoned apple in the story is also a direct reference to the Norse apples of immortality which were guarded by the goddess Idun and gave the gods and goddesses eternal youth. In the 'Snow White' story the apple is used to put Snow White to sleep but it also puts her in a state of suspended animation, keeping her eternally youthful until she is kissed and awoken by a prince.

Days of the Gods

The Norse gods are best commemorated today in the English names for the days of the week with four of the seven days named after the Norse pantheon.

Tuesday – Tyr's Day

Wednesday – Woden's Day

Thursday – Thor's Day

Friday – Freya's day

Originally the days were named after the Greek, and then Roman, gods plus the Sun and the Moon but when the Germanic peoples adopted the daily calendar they simply substituted the Greco-Roman deities for the corresponding gods and goddesses from the Norse pantheon. Although for some reason they kept Saturn for Saturday and were content to keep the Moon and Sun for Monday and Sunday respectively.

Freya's Day and Unlucky 13

The English tradition of bad luck being connected to black cats and the number thirteen is a direct reaction to the Celtic Christian rejection of the pagan mythologies, which spread throughout Ireland and Scotland thanks to Viking marauders in the 9th and 12th centuries.

The day Friday is named after the Norse goddess Freya whose sky-chariot was thought to be pulled by a group of fire cats, and the number 13 is sacred to her. Freya is associated strongly with magic and so is easily cast as an evil witch. This is why many people in the United Kingdom consider Friday the 13th to be particularly unlucky especially for travel. However in other parts of Europe it is considered a very auspicious and fortunate date.

CHAPTER SEVEN

Nature Spirits

THE CELTIC DIVINITIES

〜〜

THE DAY was dark and shrouded in a heavy, drizzling mist as Crunniuc trudged out to his field to bring in his horses. He hurried his step and hopped over the low stone wall that separated his crops from his horse pastures. He sighed, why were they never right at the gate when he came for them? Suddenly Crunnic stopped dead still, in the mist he could make out a human form standing near his best horse.

Crunniuc lifted his cudgel and strode over to the figure, but as he approached the mist lifted slightly and he saw not a horse thief, but the most beautiful flamed-haired woman gently stroking his mare.

The woman saw Crunniuc and as she smiled the sky cleared and she was bathed in the golden glow of a bright sunny day.

Mural on Dublin Street, Desmond Kinney 1974

'I'm sorry,' she said, her voice smooth as honey, 'I did not mean to upset you. I know life has been hard since your wife died.'

Crunniuc's eyes filled with tears at the mention of his dearly departed and the woman reached out and took his hand in hers. Her compassion and kindness filled his heart and chased away his sadness.

'I have not seen you before in the village,' he said finally after they had stood in silence for several minutes.

'No, I am not from the village, you should return to your home now,' the woman said.

Crunniuc furrowed his brow but something in her tone compelled him to turn and walk back towards his house.

As Crunniuc opened his front door he heard water splashing in his kitchen and the sound of footsteps moving to and from the larder. Confused, he stepped into the kitchen to find the woman from the field standing by his preparation bench, rolling pastry for a pie. She looked up and smiled at him as though her being there was the most natural thing in the world and, strangely, Crunnic felt that it was. It never occurred to him that he did not even know her name.

One morning when Crunniuc was going into the field he saw his new wife running amongst the horses. She was so fast she was almost a blur, lapping the paddock three times before she turned and sprinted towards the house.

Crunniuc hid behind the barn as his wife ran past. He had already suspected that this lovely woman was no ordinary mortal and was now convinced he may indeed be in love with a Fae.

A few months later the King of Ulster announced a great race taking place in the nearby village.

'Please do not go to the race, Husband,' the woman said. 'I feel uneasy about it. Stay here with me as I am heavy with child.'

Crunniuc scooped her into his arms and pulled her down on his lap, kissing her fondly. 'I have to take the crops in to market', he said. 'I would be foolish not to check in on the race while I am there. And who knows, maybe I may win a small wager and return with gold in my pocket.'

'I cannot forbid you, but I make one request. Do not mention me at the gathering. Not that I am here nor anything about me. There will be bad consequences if you do.'

The day of the race came and Crunniuc excitedly kissed his wife goodbye on the lips and again on her swollen belly.

'I'll be back by nightfall', he promised before heading out to the village.

The atmosphere at the race was electric. People had come from all the villages and farms around to see the king and his famed Arabian stallions. The king, proud and boastful loudly claimed that nothing on Earth was faster than his great horses.

Without thinking Crunniuc called out, 'my wife is faster than your horse!'

The whole crowd went silent and the king stared over at Crunniuc, astounded.

'What did you say?'

'My wife can run faster than either of your so-called champions,' he hardly believed he was saying the words, but they fell out of his mouth before he even realised he was going to say them.

The king's men surrounded Crunniuc and brought him roughly to the king.

'Your wife, you say?', the king said incredulously.

'Go and get this man's wife and bring her here. Tell her if she does not come I will hang her husband from the willow tree as a liar.'

The soldiers set out immediately to gather Crunniuc's wife and he was imprisoned in a nearby stable until her arrival.

The sound of the soldiers returning both gladdened and terrified Crunniuc. As he was brought out into the arena he saw his heavily pregnant wife sitting on the soldier's carriage. She looked strained and anxious but upon seeing him relief broke out on her face.

'Your husband says you can outrun my champion horse,' the king called to her. 'Is your husband a liar?'

The woman shook her head. 'I am well with child, your majesty. I will happily race your horse next year, but for now I beg you to leave me be.'

'Is your husband a liar?', the king repeated.

The woman shook her head. 'My husband is no liar.'

The king frowned. 'You are telling me that you can outrun a horse? This I have to see.'

'Please, your majesty, wait until my children are born. I will race then. But I do not wish to harm them in this.'

The king waved her away. 'You will race my horse now, or I shall have you and your husband executed for dishonesty.'

The crowd were silent, watching this woman placed next to the mighty creature. The poor wench didn't stand a chance. Crunniuc himself was racked with shame and guilt at putting his beloved in such a terrible situation.

The king called the race and his huge stallion took off in a flurry of dust and sweat. But the woman was running too, keeping up, length for length with the animal.

The king gasped seeing this common farm girl run faster than any mortal should be able to.

The rider on the horse kicked it forward, urging it to go faster but the woman stayed right by its side until the finish line came into sight. Then, with a sudden spurt of energy, she pushed forward, overtaking the horse and rider and crossing the line several feet ahead of them.

The crowd burst into hollers and applause, completely bewildered and amazed by what they had just seen. The horse covered in thick foam and sweat snorted angrily, reared up and threw its rider, before stopping exhausted by the far fence.

The woman collapsed in the dirt and started screaming as her contractions began. Even in her pain she looked up at the king who was staring down at her in anger and bewilderment. Crunniuc tore loose from the soldiers who were holding him and ran to his wife, who was now hunched over in agony.

With a mighty scream the woman gave birth to a pair of infants who Crunniuc wrapped in his coat and held close to his chest. The woman, exhausted and bloody, looked up at the king who had watched the whole event in stunned silence.

'You are a cruel and heartless man to make me run for your amusement. But I am no ordinary woman. I am Macha, goddess of Fury and spirit of the horses. Your cruelty here towards me and all women will haunt you and all your kin. For nine times nine generations all the Kings of Ulster will suffer my curse, to be wracked by the agony of childbirth just when they need their strength the most.'

With that she took her children from Crunniuc and disappeared, never to be seen again. For hundreds of years the Kings of Ulster suffered from Macha's curse and their realm was overrun and destroyed by the High Kings of the West.

❧

The myth of Macha forms one of the key stories in the mythological cycle of Celtic myths and reflects many of the key tenets of Celtic mythology. The secret power and wrath as well as kindness and loving spirit of women is an important aspect of this myth and one that is repeated several times across the collection of stories of the Celtic legends.

The earliest of the Celtic legends came from Ireland, and later Wales, before being adopted throughout the British Isles. The Irish traditional myths are broken into four specific collections of stories refered to as 'Cycles'. Each 'Cycle' reflects a particular time in Irish mythic history.

The first of these — 'The Mythological Cycle' is the one that focuses the most specifically on Celtic deities known as the Tuatha Dé Danan, or children of Danu, the original

Macha Curses the Men of Ulster by Eleanor Hull, The Boys' Cuchulain'
1902

Celtic Earth goddess. The Tuatha De Danan arrived in Ireland as a rolling mist, which enveloped the land of Eire (modern-day Ireland.) This probably related to the arrival of the Vikings in Ireland, who would burn great fires which would envelope the land in smoke.

'The Mythological Cycle' is focused on the creator goddess Danu and her son Dagda, who is considered the father of all the later gods. Goddess power was key in the matriarchal Celtic tribes and this was reflected in the use of cauldrons, as a symbol of the female womb, a key element in these stories.

The second group of tales, 'The Ulster Cycle' and the fourth Cycle, 'Fenian', were more like *Boy's Own* adventure stories featuring the great Celtic heroes Cuchulain and, in the later stories, Finn MacCumhail who shared many of the attributes of the later mythical King Arthur. These two heroes were later adopted into Scottish and British tales as well as featured in the tales from the Isle of Man.

The third cycle – called 'The Historical Cycle' tells the tales of legendary kings and it is believed by some that from these stories the legendary King Arthur of the Britons emerged.

The first known written records of the Celtic myths appeared in *The Historia Regum Britanniae* by Geoffrey of Monmonth in 1130 CE which retold the Irish mythological cycles of Ulster and Fenian in a fictional history of the mythical King Arthur. Later the Welsh *Mabinogion*, dated around 1100 CE, an anthology of 11 Celtic mythological tales, although it is believed it was probably a collection from previous manuscripts.

Despite the focus on male heroes, it is clear that it was the Celtic goddesses who held the balance of power in the Celtic pantheon. The Triple goddess, Mother/Maiden/Crone entity formed the basis of most ritualised worship and it was the females who were the guardians of magic and prophesy. Cerriwyn, the Crone manifestation of the Triple goddess was famed for her magical cauldron from which she created life, potions and food to help legendary heroes and kings.

Rites and Rituals

Although today people connect Celtic religions only with Druids, the Celtic rites were performed by three groups, all of which had very different roles.

The Druids, best translated as 'priests', performed the key religious festivals and sacred tree rites. The word Druid itself means 'knowing the oak tree' and the Druids' rituals were focused around forests and natural seasons.

The Bards, or storytellers, were also important spiritual practitioners. Writing and poetry was sacred to the Celts, who had several gods and goddesses who watched over writers and poets. The Runic or Celtic alphabet was seen as being created by the Celtic god Ogma. Bards were the storytellers and created and spread the stories of the great gods and goddesses across the continent, explaining how the religion became so popular across such a vast area. They would be more like the modern version of monks today.

The other key authorities of Celtic worship were the seers, known as the Vates. These were the holders of magical knowledge and prophecy. In later Celtic stories the practice of magic was transferred to the Druids, who became synonymous with wizards and witches in post Christian times. The wizard Merlin, often referred to as a Druid, was most probably a Vate in the old religion.

Celtic rituals, being nature-based, did not use man-made temples but rather Druids would perform rites in forests or woods, usually around a particularly important sacred tree.

Places such as Stonehenge and Avebury in England have been called Druidic temples by modern druid practitioners, but it is more likely that they were edifices for specific festivals such as Beltane or Lughnasadh.

We still celebrate pagan ceremonies

Christmas day was established not on the birthday of the Christian prophet Jesus — who has been documented as being born in late January not December. The festival of Christmas lines up more clearly with the Druidic celebration of yule, or winter Solstice in December of each year. This was a time sacred to the Celtic god of rebirth, The Dadhga or Great Father.

The inclusion of fir trees in the festivities was also an accommodation of Gallic Druidic tree worship into the Christian religious rituals and even the character of Santa Claus has elements of the Celtic god of plenty who would bestow gifts on those who pleased him.

Celtic Celebrations

The Celtic calendar was split into two equal halves of the year – the bringing of darkness known as Samahain usually around November 1st and the bringing of light, known as Beltane, now celebrated as May Day.

Within each half of the year there would be smaller festivals; Imboc which fell at the beginning of February and Lughnasadh which was celebrated on August 1.

Samahain means 'end of summer' and was a festival marking the beginning of the first day of winter when life would start to wither and die. The Celts did rituals of protection during this time and magic invocations were used to end anything that was seen as negative or unwanted from the past year. It was also seen as a time when it was possible to communicate with the other side. Young men would often stand guard all night to protect their families from the faeries and malevolent creatures who could travel across the two worlds on this night. Often Celtic families would put out treats or offerings for those who travelled from the otherworld in an effort to stop them from doing any trickery or mischief against them in the night. This is where the modern tradition of Halloween and trick-or-treat comes from.

Imbolc is a ritual celebrating the bringing in of the milk of cows and sheep. An important food source for the Celts, milk was not available year round and only after the birth of the lambs and calves. Imbolc rituals included pouring milk or cream onto the ground for a blessing to nurture and nourish the Earth through which all bounties were given.

Beltane celebrates the god Bel, the sun god and bringer of light. Two great fires were lit from the sacred branches of willow or rowan and the livestock herded between them, the sacred smoke said to purify and protect them for the next year. It was a popular date for handfastings (marriages) as well as fertility rites. Hawthorne was left on or across doorways so anyone who passed the threshold would bring in good fortune in the coming year and this is where the tradition of carrying someone across the threshold after marriage comes from.

Lughnasadh (Lammas) was the first of the true harvest festivals named in honour of the great god of all skills, Lugh, who was the chief god of the harvest. Lughnasadh was usually celebrated with athletic games and competitions enjoyed by both men and women. In Celtic traditions women were openly encouraged to be competitive and strong, possibly because of the Celts' connections with the Norse gods and goddesses which had influenced them during the Norse invasions centuries earlier.

Smaller Festivals

Yule Dec 21 – winter solstice or longest night of the year was celebrated as the eve of the birth of the sun god, who would be born and then grow to bring light once again to the dark wintery lands. The date of mid-winter yule explains why the European Christian celebration of Christmas, or Christ's birth, was moved to December 25 to capitalise on what was already a popular festival day.

Vernal Equinox March 21 — is celebrated in spring when the day and night were equally long. Symbolising a balance

Green Man Foliate head decoration, UK

in nature, these days were sacred to the Druids and were
celebrated with feasts and sun rituals.

Midsummer's day June 21 – is the longest day of the year;
midsummer was a time of rejoicing and usually celebrated
with picnics, games and bonfires.

Autumn Equinox — Like the vernal equinox, this day was
sacred, as both light and dark were equal. It was seen as the
day of the waning of the goddess, who was seen as light
and kindness, to make way for the time of the god who was
darker and more fearsome in his attitude. Rituals of thanks
were given to the goddess for her bounty over the summer
and the darker gods were placated with sacrifices and rituals
throughout the autumn and winter months.

Important Tuatha Dé Danan (Celtic Deities)

Name and Origin	Rules	Myths and Info
Bel *The Shining One* Welsh	God of fire and horses	Welsh god adopted by the Romans in the 3rd century BC. The Italian city of Aquileia was dedicated to Bel.
Blodeuwedd Welsh	Maiden of the triptych – symbolising innocence and freedom	Symbolised with an owl, like other great maiden goddesses, Athena and Ishtar, who both had owl totems.
Brighid *Brigit* *Brid* Gaelic	Writing, craft, scholarship, midwifery and inspiration	Reimagined as St Brigid, she was cast as a slave who had to reject the Druids. St Brigid is the saint of midwives and offspring but lost her more active roles as a scholar and craftswoman under the Christian ideology.
Caillech Welsh	Triple goddess Crone, goddess of disease and plague	Not seen as evil but rather as the goddess through whom those suffering from disease or plague could find release.

Cernunnos – Wales **Green Man –** Britannia **Oak Lord –** Ireland **Sucellus** – Gaul	Nature, virility and harvest	Portrayed with horns or antlers and the body of a goat, he formed the basis for the devil in Christianised UK.
Ceridwen *Cerriwyn* Gaelic	Prophesy and magic	Her cauldron was a symbol of the uterus and its connection to divine creation. It was later linked to evil and witchcraft, by Christians.
The Dagda *The Good God* *Father of All* Welsh	God of plenty, arts, music, magic and prophesy and regeneration	Brought blessings and plenty to all who worshipped him.
Danu Welsh	The originating mother goddess	She is mother to the Dagda (father of all) and one of the earliest known deities in the Celtic pantheon.
Epona – Britannia *The Great Mare* **Rhiannon –** Welsh **Macha** – Irish	Goddess of horses	Embraced by the invading Roman armies who gave offerings to her to protect their valuable cavalry horses.

Lugh Welsh	Mother element of the triple goddess symbolising abundance and fertility	The triple goddess was common in European mythologies until the monotheism religions erased women from the divine world.
Mare – Welsh **Caer Ibormeith** – Irish	Goddess of dreams and sleep	Would bring bad dreams to the wicked. As Caer Ibormeith she was a swan whose song lulled those to a peaceful rest after a hard day.
The Morrigan Britannia Wales Scotland Ireland	Goddess of fertility, war, death and fate but was also known as the goddess of revenge	Most feared of the Celtic deities, she often took the form of a black raven to keep an eye on all those who may trespass against nature.
Ogma – Gaul	God of writing	Credited with inventing the Druidic language and alphabet or runes.

Where did all the Faeries go?

As Christian monks began collecting and recording the stories of the Celtic gods and goddesses and incorporating them into other stories, they began subtly changing the

meanings and metaphors of the deities to incorporate more Christian traditions.

Many of the great Celtic gods were transformed into legendary kings and the goddesses started to be written out of the tales, often little more than love interests for these powerful new kings.

The nature spirits were relegated into the arena of folk tales and quickly lost their divine status. These supernatural creatures became the stuff of faerytales and rural superstitions and were not taken seriously by the Catholic and later English Protestant churches of the

United Kingdom. Despite this, in several areas of the British Isles belief in these faery creatures remained strong, and their stories continued to be told through literature, films, television and art.

Odd Fact

The Catholic saint, St Patrick, is believed to have received a vision that the Celtic myths of his homeland must be recorded and respected. He instructed the monks to start recording these tales which prior to the Catholic translations only existed in oral form and within some latin works.

CHAPTER EIGHT

Don't Disappoint Us!

THE GODS AND GODDESSES OF PRE-COLUMBIAN AMERICA

❧

THE GREAT gods of the Aztecs had once been mortals, living on the land and creating all that was good and bountiful –the maize, the forest, the animals, and the rivers. The great gods created it all.

After a while the feathered serpent god, Quetzalcoatl created humankind, whom he showered with gifts of food and water. The people were cold in the darkness so Quetzalcoatl took to the sky and became a bright burning sun to give his people light and warmth. Yet from his vantage point he saw that these were stupid, vain and feeble creatures that he had created.

Disappointed, he flew down from the sky and left the people to die in the cold and misery.

Once all of Quetzalcoatl's people were dead the god Tezcatlipoca, thinking he could create a better version of humankind, gave life to a new breed of people, faster, stronger and more intelligent. Once he was satisfied he too took up the place of the sun and shone down on his new creations.

But these humans proved weak and unable to survive the world in which they had been created and Tezcatlipoca, growing weary of their mewing and helplessness rained fire upon them, destroying them instantly.

The gods Tlaloc and Ehecatl jeered the two creator gods, ridiculing their useless creations.

'If you can do better please go ahead', Quetzalcoatl responded.

Tlaloc, and then Ehecatl, each took up the role of sun and creator god, each believing their version of humanity would be better than the last.

But both were again disappointed with the simple weak beings they created who could not fight, fly, nor exist under water. So the two younger gods each admitted that they had failed and again plunged the world into darkness, releasing the dreaded Tzitzimimeh, fallen star creatures with savage bloodlust to devour the remaining humans in the darkness.

Quetzalcoatl pondered their failures and, not one to give up on an idea, he was determined to have one last attempt at creating a strong, resilient and fearless tribe of creatures who would make him proud with their courage and dominance.

Quetzalcoatl wanted to ensure that these new people were the strongest they could be so the fearsome goddess Cihuacoatl, who was wise in magic, retrieved the sacred

Quetzalcoatl from the Codex Borgia 16th Century

bones of the previous humans and mixed them with
corn and Quetzalcoatl's own blood to shape the bodies.
Quetzalcoatl then gave them the sacred breath of life …
creating what he hoped would be worthy beings.

   'If these humans prove true then the sun must remain in
the heavens for them. One of us must sacrifice our mortal
body and become the Sun for eternity', Quetzalcoatl told
the gods as they watched the new people emerge from the
dust and bones.

But the gods, having already been disappointed by the previous people were hesitant to sacrifice their own mortal lives. There was a long wait and finally two of the smaller gods stepped forward.

Tecciztecatl was a proud and greedy god and the others were surprised that he would put himself forward. Tecciztecatl however knew that sacrificing his mortal body to become the sun would make him immortal and possibly more powerful than the stronger gods who currently reigned.

The other volunteer was the quiet and humble god Nanauatl. When asked why he had volunteered he replied, 'Our job as creators and gods is to look over and protect our creations. This job will be a sacred duty.'

The two gods were purified and asked to make a sacrifice.

Tecciztecatl brought gold, turquoise and bright coral to dazzle the eye, although only a fraction of that which he had amassed over his lifetime. Nanauatl had no gold or treasures to offer so he slit open his arm and dripped his blood into a bowl and presented that as his offering.

'Gold and coral are pretty and expensive, but Tecciztecatl is not really losing much by giving it to us. Nanauatl is offering his own spirit, a part of himself which is worthier than a thousand gold pieces,' Quetzalcoatl remarked.

The gods made a big fire, which burned for four days and four nights until it was almost as high as the heavens. The gods declared that whichever one could safely jump over the flames had the power and strength to become the sun.

Nanauatl and Tecciztecatl looked at the fire nervously. It was flaring brightly and the heat scorched their skin from several feet away. Running towards the flames would be suicide.

Taking a deep breath, Tecciztecatl pushed Nanauatl aside roughly and ran towards the flame, determined to be the first to jump over it. But as he approached he stopped short, and backed away.

'I am just warming up. Assessing the best way to gain momentum.'

The other gods allowed Tecciztecatl to try again, and again he stopped. Nanauatl said nothing, watching patiently as Tecciztecatl tried one last time. But the cowardly god could not bring himself to leap into the flames.

Quetzalcoatl, impatient now, called Tecciztecatl back to the group.

'No one can jump that', Tecciztecatl complained bitterly as he made his way back to the other gods.

Not waiting to be invited, Nanauatl stepped out of the shadows and ran soundlessly towards the fire, never hesitating or slowing his gait as he raced up and launched himself into the flames.

Tecciztecatl heard the other gods yelling their approval and his body flooded with anger at being upstaged like this. Without thinking he turned around and launched himself into the fire right after Nanauatl.

The other gods stared at the fire for a few seconds. Nothing

could be seen and they slumped back, disappointed. Suddenly a huge fireball exploded out of the fire up into the sky. Within the flames the gods saw the face of Nanauatl, now the mighty sun. Another small fireball shot up into the sky and appeared next to Nanauatl. A second sun was now in the heavens.

The heavens started to catch alight as the two Suns struggled. Their combined heat searing the people Quetzalcoatl had created. Quetzalcoatl enraged that these gods were not taking care of his new creatures, snatched up a nearby rabbit and threw it with mighty force directly into Teccizatecatl's fiery face.

Tecciztecatl recoiled and his flame started to extinguish. He tried to keep some of his fire going but to do so he had to retreat from Nanauatl. As his light faded the shape of the rabbit could be seen, burnt into Tecciztecatl's face, marking him forever.

Realising he had lost, the greedy god retreated, leaving Nanauatl alone in the sky.

The gods ordered Nanauatl to move across the sky to give relief from his heat, for even though it was not as fatal as the two Suns, the people still needed respite from this mightiest of fires.

Nanauatl the Sun shook his head. 'I am not moving until you make a commitment to be true gods. You all must give up your mortal forms and sacrifice yourselves for human kind.'

The other gods baulked at the suggestion. Give up their lives? Why should they do this? But the god Ehecatl looked at the Aztec people who Quetzalcoatl had made and saw them bearing the heat stalwartly, building great cities and dominating the lands. He saw they were worthy and nodded at the wise Nanauatl.

'This is humanity's last chance. We need to let them prove themselves on their own,' Ehecatl said.

The other gods hesitantly gave in and agreed to sacrifice their mortal selves for this new human kind.

Aztec Priest sacrifices a victim - Codex Laud 16th Century

Ehecatl tore open the chests of the gods and ripped out their hearts; one by one he threw the still beating organs into the great fire and the gods transformed into spirit. Then he turned to the men and women who had watched this great sacrifice and addressed them.

'Remember this and always know that through pain and sacrifice you show your love of us, just as we have shown our love of you in this way.'

With that he threw himself into the fire and transformed into a mighty wind, strong enough to blow the sun across the sky and give respite to the sweltering world. The new race of Aztec people pledged from that day never to disappoint the great gods who had sacrificed so much for them.

It is hard to imagine a more terrifying or violent group of deities than those who were worshipped throughout the Aztec and Toltec civilisations of what is now modern-day Mexico.

Human sacrifices were not unknown in many religions across the world, but the Aztecs brought human sacrifice up to a whole new level. Not only did they routinely sacrifice prisoners of war, slaves, women and children to their gods, they concocted some of the most bizarre, grisly and painful ways to do so.

Sacrificial victims would find themselves flayed alive and their skins worn by the priests in macabre rituals. Crying, terrified children would be offered up to Tlaloc, the god of rain and flooding, their tears collected in glass bowls and offered at the altars before the children would be drowned and left to float out into the rivers towards the sea.

The moon goddess Coyolxauhqui was honoured by amputating the limbs from the sacrificial victim and then decapitating him and tossing his head up onto her altar, in this way mimicking the death of the goddess in her legend, where she was slaughtered in revenge for her attack upon her pregnant mother, Coatlicue. Coyolxauhqui was set upon by her half-brother and torn limb from limb before her severed head was thrown into the sky to create the moon.

All religions had some form of punishment built into their belief systems, but to the Aztecs there were no righteous few who would survive the wrath of an angry god. If displeased, the Aztec gods would not just erupt a volcano or hold back the harvest for that year, they would remove the sun from the heavens and unleash the horrifying fallen stars, the Tzitzimimeh, who would devour any who survived the cold darkness.

The Aztecs had to appease these spirits to ensure that they were not another lost civilisation, created and then destroyed by the gods because they had failed to impress them with their bravery, violence, sacrifice and dominance.

Important Aztec Deities

Name	Function	Myths and worship
Centeotl	God of corn	Son of Tlazolteotl and husband of Xochiquetzal.
Chicomecoatl	Goddess of food and produce Goddess of fertility	Every September, she received a sacrifice of a young decapitated girl whose blood was poured on a statue and whose skin was worn by a priest.
Cihuacoatl	Motherhood and fertility goddess. Goddess for those who die in childbirth	A fierce and vicious woman depicted with a skull-like face, she is said to haunt crossroads waiting to steal unsupervised children.

Name	Function	Myths and worship
Coatlicue	Mother goddess of the Earth who gives birth to all celestial things	An insatiable cannibal that consumes every living thing. She is death and destruction as much as the birth of the universe.
Coyolxauhqui	Moon goddess	Prevented from killing her mother Coatlicue by her brother who ripped her limbs apart and threw her head into the sky to create the Moon.
Ehecatl	An aspect of Quetzalcoatl god of the wind	Legend has it he fell in love with a human girl and then bestowed the gift of love on all humankind so that they could feel its joy.

Name	Function	Myths and worship
Huehueteotl	Old god, god of fire	One of the earliest gods worshipped in pre-Columbian Mexico his main purpose is lost in history though he is linked to ruling and warriors.
Huitzilopochtli	God of war and victory. Represented as the sun winning a daily war against darkness, defeating the Moon and the stars	Victims, usually opponents caught in war, were decapitated and their heads strung up on a great rack below Huitzilopochtli's temple.
Ixtlilton	God of healing, feasting and games	He was honoured with the playing of games – some played using severed human heads. He also represented hallucinogenic herbs which were used in many of the Aztec healing and religious rituals.

Name	Function	Myths and worship
Mictlantecuhtli and Mictecacihuatl	God and goddess of the underworld	Ruled the lowest level of the underworld called Mictlan.
Mixcoatl	God of the Milky Way and god of the hunt	Sacrifices: a woman's head would be beaten in with a rock, her throat cut and her head chopped off. The murderer would then himself be sacrificed, having his heart ripped out of his chest. This was supposed to be a great honour.
Nannuncatl *Nanauatzin*	The Sun god	He sacrificed himself in a pit of fire to become the Sun and give light and warmth to the people.
Omacatl	God of feasting and happiness	Worshipped by the wealthy, this god was honoured by the eating of corn replicas and sexual orgies, which could continue for weeks.

Name	Function	Myths and worship
Ometeotl	Dual male and female god/goddess who was one of the original gods brought through from the Toltecs	Mentioned in many of the writings as a supreme god/goddess. There is no evidence of practical worship of this deity.
Ometochtli	God of drunkenness	A trickster god who leads the 400 rabbit gods of drunkenness, a drunk rabbit army if you will.
Quetzalcoatl.	Feathered serpent Creator god	The best known of the ancient gods, his symbolic connection to snakes echoes the importance of that animal across most ancient civilisations.
Tepeyollotl	God of earthquakes and jaguars	A fairly minor deity worshipped in remote regions of Mexico where earthquakes were common.

Name	Function	Myths and worship
Tezcatlipoca	God of night, temptation, beauty, sorcery and war	His mirror, usually depicted on his chest or foot, reflects what it sees and rewards or punishes as appropriate.
Tlaloc	God of rain and water	Drowned children appeased this most fearsome god and prevented floods, mudslides and drownings.
Tonatiuh	Sun god	Aztecs believed that several gods tried and failed at being the Sun over the eons of time and with the failure of each Sun the human race was destroyed.
Tzitzimimeh	Star goddesses, fertility, protection of women	Although protectors, the Tzitzimimeh were also credited with devouring all the previous humans who disappointed the gods.

Name	Function	Myths and worship
Xipe Totec	Life–death–rebirth, agriculture, the west, disease, spring, goldsmiths and the seasons	Xipe Totec flayed his own skin in order to give food, in the form of maize seed, to the people so they could flourish. He is honoured by flaying victims alive.
Xiuhtecuhtli	God of life after death	Honoured with the usual human sacrifice burnt in a fire, symbolising the light brought by Xiuhtecuhtli into the darkness of death.

CHAPTER NINE

The Voodoo You Do So Well

WEST AFRICA AND THE VOODOO LOA

❧

THE GODDESS Oshun rose from her morning bath in the great salty sea, water dripping off her ebony skin and feeding rivers and lakes across the grand expanse of the African plains. The animals and people of the savannahs refreshed themselves by her waterways and she ensured they had cool respite from the fierceness of her brother the Sun as he made his way across the sky.

And so it was for many years, the people making their offering to the great goddess who maintained the flow of life-giving water. Until one day the offerings did not come. Oshun looked about her but the village was empty.

Feeling a stab of apprehension, Oshun noticed strange tracks from the huts, as though the tribe had left their homes in a large group, herded towards the faraway beaches.

Papa Legba Loa Symbol

Oshun followed the tracks and as she walked over the mountain she saw her people shivering and frightened on the golden sands. A group of others, pale as milk were shouting and herding the tribe onto a great wooden ship, the likes of which Oshun knew belonged far across the seas, but not here on the isles of West Africa.

The boats, once full of their human cargo, set off and Oshun followed, diving into the sea. Her legs turning into a sleek scaly tail as she hurried after her people, unsure what to do to help them.

The people saw their goddess and cried out for her, singing songs of worship, but the pale people beat them and told them to stop singing.

The men and women were taken down into the bowels of the ship and Oshun felt herself weakening as her people stopped their singing and could not make their offerings.

Still she pushed on. A great storm came and washed Oshun away from the ship, and she saw other crafts, large and full of African tribespeople. Some called out for her or the other gods, but soon it became silent and Oshun lost track of her people.

For many months she swam through the oceans, searching for them. But the ships she found were dark on the bottom of the sea, her people drowned. She blessed the bodies and promised that their ancestors would not forget them, but knew it would be hard to keep their spirits alive when they had been lost so far from home.

Exhausted and desolate, Oshun caught sight of land ahead, and on the wind she heard the faintest echo of the old songs, the old stories.

She swam urgently towards the shore and there she saw people, dressed in rags and tilling the fields or reaping the great harvests of sugar cane. They sang the old songs but they had new words. The language they spoke was strange, guttural and unfamiliar.

Oshun emerged from the sea, bringing the life waters to the people. They drew back from her. In the years they had forgotten their great goddess. She tried to tell them stories of the gods back in Africa, but they only shook their heads.

'We believe in the one great god now', they told her. Oshun cried and her tears were salty and poisoned the lands. The people begged her not to do so as the masters would beat them if the harvests did not come.

Oshun went back into the sea, but she could not leave her people, even though they had not welcomed her.

She listened as the masters told her people stories of this new god and his resurrection and of his saintly mother and the virgin birth. She heard the tales of the terrible flood and God's wrath upon those who did not respect his name, and the stories of the saints who had sacrificed themselves to bring kindness and love into the land.

She listened and she learned, and then she came to them as a young woman, impossibly beautiful and strong and told them that the great god had sent her to protect them, like their own personal saint.

The people, craving some sign of love from this new god, embraced this woman and named her Erzulie, a spirit of love and protection.

She stayed with them in their huts at night and told them the stories of the old African Gods but she gave them new names, incorporating the tales of the new god into the stories of the old. She told them of the great sky serpent, Damballah who brought the rains and his wife Aya the rainbow, whose presence after a storm promised better days to come if they kept the faith. She taught them the old songs and she learnt the new words and the people began to worship her again, feeling themselves forsaken no longer.

The people started to remember their ancient ways, they started to sing the songs and make the offerings. Oshun grew stronger here and when the white masters came to preach their gospels she told the people to call her the black Madonna, so that the white people would know that they had not abandoned the new god.

The people understood and would weave the stories of the Madonna and the saints into their ancient tales, creating the Loa, or Voodoo deities who watched over the slaves of Haiti and helped them find the strength to endure, and finally overcome, their slavery.

❧

The Loa and the Saints

Haitian Voodoo tradition incorporated the Haitian deities or Loa into the half-understood stories of the Catholic saints, creating a truly unique religious pantheon that took from both the African and European religious traditions.

Yet despite these similarities the Haitian Loa added a distinctly Afro-Caribbean aspect to the rituals and stories. They became a way for the African people of Haiti and Jamaica, Cuba and Brazil to see themselves and their suffering reflected in the stories of their deities.

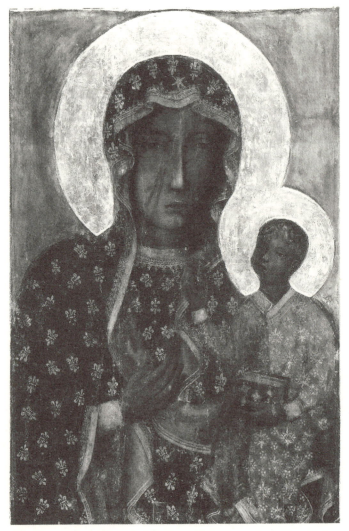

The goddess Erzulie represented as the Black Madonna

The Loas or Voodoo deities are broken into two specific groups which reflected the unique history and traditions of West African slaves in Haiti.

The Rada Loa represent the stability and warmth of the sun and the joy and freedoms of Africa. Rada Loas are more likely to originate from West African gods and traditional folk tales and tend to be kinder, warmer and more loving.

The Petro are the Loa forged from suffering, fire and slavery. They represent the rage, horror and delirium of enslavement and revolution. They are not negative so much as more violent and dangerous Loa who are invoked when great strength, dark magic and trickery is needed.

Both Petro and Rada Loa incorporate many of the stories and traditions of the Christian gods which Haitian slaves were forced to adopt after their removal from Africa.

Baron Samedi, one of the most well known of the Voodoo Petro Loa is a dark and sinister figure. He demands his worshippers become zombies, mindless slaves bent to his will. Those who gain the favour of Baron Samedi will have power and riches but he is a cruel and unpredictable ally. Baron Samedi was a deity who represented the power and terror of the slave traders and plantation owners who controlled the life and death of their slaves.

Loa do not seem too concerned about how their magic is used by their supplicants, offering both curses and blessings in equal measure as long as they felt the reward or punishment was deserved. Erzulie was often called upon by women who wanted protection from, or revenge upon their abusive husbands, as well as single men and women looking for true love.

Magic, transcendence and possession by the Loa are key elements in the Voodoo traditions, and are part of the reason why the idea of Voodoo is considered more a superstition than a religion, as well as its rejection by the greater Christian populations of the Americas.

Rites and Rituals

Voodoo is practised today across central America in Jamaica, Haiti and Cuba. In the southern states of the United States of America (USA) the practice is often referred to as Hoodoo and in other areas of the USA the term 'Santería' is now used to cover many of the original West African practices on which voodoo was based.

The rituals and ceremonies vary across the different regions but most are conducted by a high Voodoo priest called a Houdan, or priestess referred to as a Mamba. Traditionally there were no specific temples for Voodoo rituals as the original practitioners performed their rites in secret in personal houses, sugar fields, cemeteries or forests.

Fete for a Loa

This is a traditional ceremony or Voodoo party dedicated to a specific Loa, although it can also be used to celebrate a number of Loa or call upon all the Loa for dedication and thanks.

The fete usually begins with drumming, dancing and singing, normally in a public place involving the whole voodoo community.

These ceremonies are scheduled to correlate with Catholic Saint days, as many of the Loa, are associated with the Christian saints. The Serpent Loa Damaballah for example is linked with St Patrick's Day as the snake god symbolises the snakes removed from Ireland by the Catholic saint.

Trances and Possessions

The most unique aspect of Voodoo is the use of transcendence trances to connect to or be possessed by the Loa. These possessions usually happen in public rituals as the energy required to achieve a sacred trance is exhaustive and requires a group of people all committed to the task.

Each Loa manifests differently and demands different actions of their vessel during possession. The possession by a Loa is seen as sacred and can only be achieved by someone who has been initiated into the ways of Voodoo. However any Voodoo practitioner can achieve possession through dance rituals, ingesting the correct herbal potions and submitting themselves up to the Loa as a vessel. Once possessed the human experience can be enjoyed for a time

Voodoo Sky Serpent – Damballah

by the Loa and the human is then rewarded by the Loa with
heightened magical powers, good fortune, love or wealth.

Private Rituals and Practices

Many of the offerings and connections begin with a
worshipper going to see a Mamba or Houdan for a specific
service or engaging in private daily rituals to show their love
and fidelity for a particular Loa.

If a worshipper wishes to gain help from a Houdan
or Mamba they must pay a private fee. Common services
include divinations or readings where the Mamba or
Houdan will read cards, bones or candle wax formations to
help Voodoo believers commune with the Loa and solve
problems, or ease worries.

Mambas and Houdans can also be requested to create
spells or potions called Wanga or Trabago to assist the client
to achieve a goal. There is no restriction on the type or target
of the magic requested as long as the request comes with
the relevant payment and offerings to the Loa who would
grant it. Love spells, vengeance spells and wealth spells are
particularly popular although curses towards rivals are also
requested.

Houdans and Mambos can also conjure spirits and
ghosts to perform specific actions for the client. This sort
of ritual is considered very dangerous because the spirits
are powerful and are often unhappy to be enslaved into the
service of a mortal.

Loa marriages are common practices where a practitioner chooses their sacred Loa, and completes a ceremonial marriage to the deity. People may do this to gain protection or a stronger connection with their Loa. Sometimes a marriage is demanded to take place by the Loa through dreams or possession rituals of the practitioner.

Baths and cleanliness are also ritualised in Voodoo with people taking spiritual baths in blessed water, which is created by the Mamba or Houdan. Baths are also used to heal illnesses and create a sense of wellbeing for the bather. They are not unlike the traditional practices of aromatherapy or Bach flower remedies that are used in alternative medicine and are also linked to the Christian ceremony of baptism.

Despite its reputation and the ability for the Mambas and Houdans to connect to and confer with the power of spirits, Voodoo is mostly a peaceful, reverential practice where practitioners align themselves to different Loas to attain good fortune, grace and assistance in life.

Damballah Loa Symbol

Important Voodoo Loas

Name	Rules	Main Story
Agwe Rada Loa Origin: Yorba *St Ulrich*	The sea, fish, fishing, protects seafarers and fishermen	Agwe is one of the husbands of Erzulie in her form as Le Siren. In rituals he is invoked by blowing a conch shell and wrapping oneself in wet towels.
Agau Petro Loa Origin: West Africa	Thunder, lightning, earthquakes	Possession by Agau is usually violent and energetic. Those possessed by this Loa will make the sound of thunder to signal his presence.
Ayezan Rada Loa Origin: West Africa *Celtic Mother Goddess*	Markets, public places, doors and barriers	A loving Loa who cares greatly for her devotees. She punishes only in order to stop mistakes being made twice. Invoked through the offering of a russet ox or goat.
Ayida Rada Loa Origins: West Africa *Leprecauns*	Rainbow, wealth, mothers, compassion	Her job is to hold up the earth. Vodouns believe if she can be captured in her rainbow form great wealth will be bestowed by her.

Name	Rules	Main Story
Bakulu Petro Loa Origin: West Africa	Forests, wild animals	Never invoked for possession — offerings are made to him in woods and forested areas to keep areas safe from his wrath.
Baron Samedi Petro Loa Origin: *Slave owners*	Death	Baron's permission is needed to speak to the dead. He is invoked for those with terminal illnesses. Funeral ash, cemeteries dirt and skulls of dead animals call him.
Brise Rada Loa Origin: West Africa *Nature Spirit*	Protector of hills and forests	Although frightening in appearance, Brise is a kind god who loves children. He can be invoked through the offering of a speckled hen.
Damballah Rada Loa Origin: Yorba *St Patrick*	Fertility (with his wives Erzulie and Ayida), rain and human sexuality	Damballah calms others and is therefore invoked at the end of ceremonies or during times of great stress. He can be called through the offering of eggs, which are his favourite food.

Name	Rules	Main Story
Erzulie Rada Loa Origin: Yorba *Oshun Mother Mary, Black Madonna*	Beauty, love, protection of women, vengeance, the sea, waterways, dreams, aspirations. wealth and riches are also her domain	Invoked for love spells, vengeance or fertility; inspires creativity and prophetic dreams. Possession by Erzulie usually ends in tears as she takes on all the sorrows of the world. She is highly sexual and virginal, kind and destructive. Invoked with her heart symbol, rich foods, jewellery and gold.
Jean Petro The spiritual head of the Petro Loa Origin: *Historical figure Jean Petro*	Resistance, force, uprisings	Jean Petro is usually only invoked for personal vengeance and by Mambas or Houdans who require strong, if unpredictable, magic.
Kalfu Petro Loa Origin: *Lucifer West African Witch Doctors*	Crossroads, black magic, evil spirits	Sits at the darkness of the crossroads, and controls the malevolent spirits of the night. A grand magician, he aides those wanting to engage in black magic. He can be a dangerous and unpredictable Loa.

Name	Rules	Main Story
Legba Rada Loa Origin: Sun god of West Africa *St Peter*	Destiny intermediary between god and humans	The original Loa of voodoo and opens the spirit gates to allow communication with the other Loa.
Loco Rada Loa Origin: West African *John the Baptist*	Medicine, healing, doctors and medical personnel, trees and vegetation	Invoked by doctors before beginning a medical procedure. He is strongly aligned with trees and invoked to resolve family, business and personal conflicts.
Ogaun Rada Loa Origin: Benin *Moses, The Christ, St Jacques*	Warriors, blacksmiths	It is said that Ogaun gave the people the strength to overthrow their slave masters in the Haitian revolt of 1804 and he is seen as a bringer of freedom. He often manifests as a wounded warrior in a Christ-like pose.
Papa Ghede Petro Loa Origin: *Lucifer*	Death, crossroads, cemeteries and keeper of secrets and erotic adventures	Possession by him is highly entertaining for others as he will often ridicule, embarrass and expose those whom he possesses.

Name	Rules	Main Story
Shango Rada Loa Origin: Yorba	Fire, justice, lightning	Shango is one of the original Loa. Invoked when one is facing an injustice or a court proceeding.

Modern Voodoo

Voodoo is still practised throughout the Caribbean, Haiti, Trinidad, Tobago, Dominica and Cuba. Its rituals have also been incorporated into folk beliefs across North America in African and Latin communities.

However in modern popular culture Voodoo is seen as a negative, evil practice used by witchdoctors and satanists.

Horror films like *White Zombie* (1932) *The Skeleton Key* (2005), *Angel Heart* and *The Serpent and The Rainbow* (1988) helped cement the voodoo tradition into the realms of horror and supernatural, yet more realistic references such as the hoodoo curses in the true crime novel and film *Midnight in the Garden of Good and Evil* and the somewhat less realistic James Bond classic *Live and Let Die*, did little to change the perception that Voodoo was only about curses, zombies and possession and not a complicated, highly spiritual religious tradition in its own right.

Voodoo Worshippers arrested, 1864 Haiti

More recently zombies lost their direct association with voodoo and the politics of slavery to become linked more with our fear of biological warfare and disease introduced in the new zombie mythologies of *The Night of the Living Dead* films and sequels and the more recent *World War Z* and *The Walking Dead* television and graphic novel franchises.

Voodoo Dolls

Voodoo dolls are possibly the most recognised element of voodoo practice around the world. They are seen as a way to inflict physical harm on a rival or enemy from a distance simply by sticking pins or sharp objects into a doll-like effigy of the person.

Although this is the popular idea, in voodoo practices dolls are used for a variety of reasons and the original idea of pins or nails comes from a west African Congolese custom of the Nkondi – a carving of a religious figure or hunter.

The Nkondi serves as a resting place for a spirit that will reward the maker by hunting down any enemies and generally protecting the properties of those who carved or own the Nkondi figure.

The Nkondi was then combined with the European practices of doll magic or poppets, which were used throughout the USA and central Americas by European witchcraft practitioners for a variety of reasons including protection, spells and curses.

The two practices were combined in Voodoo to create the voodoo doll that can be used to encourage the Loas' help in casting protective as well as cursory magic.

CHAPTER TEN

Modern Gods

꒰ ꒱

ALL OF the gods and goddesses you have met in this book speak to us from millennia ago, before many of the current gods ascended their spiritual thrones.

One may think that these difficult, amazing, frustrating, cheeky and beautiful deities have gone from us now, uncared for, lost in time and space. The truth is that throughout the world in small pockets there are still those who hold the flames for these goddesses and gods of old, performing the rituals, telling the stories and embracing the idea of a great mother, a spiritual Earth and symbolic relationship with divine beings.

Modern Druids throughout the United Kingdom enact Solstice and Equinox rituals and celebrate many of the old pagan ways. In some islands of the Mediterranean the old Hellenic and Cretan gods are remembered and offerings made. The people of Bali continue their animist traditions amidst the biggest Muslim population on Earth and despite the colonisation and Christianisation in Western Africa, Australia and the Americas some tribes still hold on to the traditional ways; and witchdoctors, elders and wise women are often called upon to perform the almost forgotten rites of magic, fortune telling and protection.

Across the world many are turning to a nature religion as they endeavour to reconnect to the spirit of the Earth. The rise of a global consciousness around environmentalism, animal welfare and conservation has seen new audiences embrace many of the old nature-based practices and spiritual teachings, incorporating the names and legends of these old deities to teach new generations that the Earth itself is something to be revered and worshipped as the mother of us all.

These gods may have retreated, shadowy in the corners of collective consciousness, but they are not lost to us, and we may still find wisdom in their stories, if we are willing to listen.

Stonehenge sunrise ritual July 2013.

Afterword

This book has been a labour of love for me.

I hope you have enjoyed reading this book and enjoy the other titles in this wonderful series, which allow us to explore the strange, hidden and mysterious worlds around us.

Until we meet again may all the gods and goddesses of past, present and future watch over and protect you.

Bibliography and Reference Guide

Bellows, Henry Adams (2004). *The Poetic Edda: The Mythological Poems.* Dover Publications.

Bjordvand, Harald, Lindeman, Fredrik, Otto (2007). *Våre arveord.* Novus.

Blanton, Richard E.; Stephen A. Kowalewski; Gary M. Feinman; Laura M. Finsten (1993) [1981]. *Ancient Mesoamerica: A Comparison of Change in Three Regions.* Cambridge University Press. Cambridge, UK:

Boone, Elizabeth Hill (2013). *Cycles of Time and Meaning in the Mexican Books of Fate.* University of Texas Press.

Budapest, Zsuzsanna (1995). *The Holy Book of Women's Mysteries.* Wingbow Press. fourth edition.

Byock, Jesse (Trans.) (2005). *The Prose Edda.* Penguin Classics.

Bulfinch, Thomas (1993). *The Golden Age of Myth and Legend;* Wordsworth Editions Great Britain

Campbell, Joseph (1991). *Primitive Mythology (The Masks of God)* Deckle Edge

Chalmers Werner, Edward Theodore (2014). *Myths and Legends of China (Traditional Chinese lore),* Start Classics.

Cheng'en, Wu and Jenner, W J F 2003; *Journey to the West (4 volumes) Foreign Language Press*

Christ, Carol P., Plaskow, Judith 2016; *Goddess and God in the World: Conversations in Embodied Theology*

Christenson, Allen J 2007 [2003]. *"Popul Vuh: Sacred Book of the Quiché Maya People" (PDF)*. Mesoweb articles. *Mesoweb: An Exploration of Mesoamerican Cultures.*

Crow, W.B 1972, *A History of Magic, Witchcraft and Occultism,* Sphere Books London

Daimler, Morgan 2016 *Pagan Portals- Gods and Goddesses of Ireland. A Guide to Irish Deities.* Amazon e book. Amazon Digital Services Pty Ltd.

David, Rosalie 2002, Religion and Magic in Ancient Egypt. Penguin. London

Davidson, H. R. Ellis 1990, *Gods and Myths of Northern Europe.* Penguin Books.

Drake, St Claire 1970. *The Redemption of Africa and Black Religion.* Institute of Positive Education. 1st Edition.

Dronke, Ursula (Trans.) 1997, *The Poetic Edda: Volume II: Mythological Poems.* Oxford University Press.

Eastman, Roger 1999, *The Ways of Religion: An Introduction to the Major Traditions.* Oxford University Press, USA; 3 edition.

Frazer, James George; 1976 *The Golden Bough, A study in comparative religion,* Macmilliam Press UK

Gaskell, G.A; 1981; *Dictonary of all Scripture and Myths,* Avenel Book, New York

George, Andrew (translator) 2010, *The Epic of Gilgamesh. The Babylonian Epic Poem and other texts in Akkadian and Sumerian.* The Folio Society

Georgoulas, Lazaros 2016. *The 10 Most famous and Most Worshipped Gods and Goddesses of the Chinese Pantheon.* Amazon E-Book

Gimbutas, Marija; Mount-Williams, Linda 1982; *The Goddesses and Gods of Old Europe: Myths and Cult Images,* New and Updated Edition, University of California Press.

Guiley, Rosemary Ellen 1991, *The Lunar Almanac,* Cynthia Piatkus Publishing, Great Britain.

Kenaz Filan (10 November 2006). *The Haitian Vodou Handbook: Protocols for Riding with the Lwa.* Inner Traditions / Bear & Co.

Kaldera, Raven, Krasskova 2012, *Neolithic Shamanism: Spiritwork in the Norse Tradition.* Destiny Books, 1st Edition.

Lesko, Barbara S 1999, *The Great Goddesses of Egypt.* University of Oklahoma Press.

Lewis, James; Chalmbers Spence, Thomas, 1913; *The Myths of Mexico and Peru: Aztec, Maya and Inca.*

Lewis-Williams, David & Pearce, David 2009, *Inside the Neolithic Mind: Consciousness, Cosmos and the Realm of the Gods* Thames and Hudson 1st Edition.

Lindow, John 2002, Norse Mythology: *A Guide to Gods, Heroes, Rituals and Beliefs.* Oxford University Press. 1st Edition.

Meeks, Dimitri; Favard-Meeks, Christine, Goshgarian G.M.(Trans) 1996 [1993], *Daily Life of the Egyptian Gods.* Cornell University Press.

McCarthy, Scott FR 1994, *People of the Circle, People of the Four Directions: A gathering of Native American Prayers, Rituals and Traditions,* Blue Dolphin Publishing.

McCoy, Edain 2002, *Celtic Myth and Magick Harness the Power of the Gods and Goddesses.* Llewellen

McCoy, Daniel 2016, *The Viking Spirit – An introduction to Norse Mythology and Religion.* CreateSpace Independent Publishing Platform.

Miller, Mary & Karl, Taube 1993, *The Gods and Symbols of Ancient Mexico and the Maya,* Thames and Hudson, London.

Momen, Moojan 2009, originally published as *The Phenomenon of Religion in 1999, Understanding Religion: A Thematic Approach,* Oneworld Publications, Oxford, UK.

Opoku, Kofi Asare 1978, *West African Traditional Religion,* FEP International Private Limited.

Parrinder, Geoffrey 2014, *West African Religion: A Study of the Beliefs and Practices of Akan, Ewe, Yoruba, Ibo, and Kindred Peoples,* Wipf & Stock.

Pennick, Nigel 1992, *The Pagan Source Book,* Random Century Group, London

Pinn, Anthony B 2005, *The African American Religious Experience in America,* Greenwood Press.

Pinch, Geraldine *2004, Egyptian Mythology: A Guide to the Gods, Goddesses, and Traditions of Ancient Egypt,* Oxford University Press.

Rhys, John 2014, *Celtic Folklore* – Welsh and Manx.

Rosenthal, Judy 1998, *Possession, Ecstasy and Law in Ewe Voodoo,* University of Virginia Press.

Shafer, Byron E (ed.) 1991, *Religion in Ancient Egypt: Gods, Myths, and Personal Practice,* Cornell University Press.

Slater, Herman (ed.) 1978, *A Book of Pagan Rituals,* Robert Hale, London.

Tuffley, David 2013, *The Essence of Buddhism.* Shambalah Dragon,1st Edition.

Tzu, Lao 2017, *Tao Te Ching: Illustrated,* Amazon E-Book Amazon Digital Services Pty Ltd.

Wong, Eva 2011, *Taoism, An Essential guide.* Shambalah Dragon. Ed. Edition

Yang, Lihui et al. 2005, *Handbook of Chinese Mythology.* Oxford University Press, New York.

Zanko, Vanda & Leonard, Miriam 2012, *Laughing with Medusa; Clasical Myth and Feminist Thought,* Oxford University Press

Websites

exemplore.com/magic/Vodou-Voodoo-The-Loa-Lwa-Spirits-of-
Voodoo-and-How-They-Can-Help-You-Voodoo-Magic

www.scribd.com/document/270981438/
Encyclopedia-of-Chinese-Pantheon

www.ancient-origins.net/human-origins-folklore/
origins-human-beings-according-ancient-sumerian-texts-0065

http://peopleof.oureverydaylife.com/description-sumerian-religious-
practices-7050.html

Illustration list for Gods and Goddesses

All images found on Wikimedia Commons and used under creative commons license.

Page vi – Page 93 – Ragnarok. Xylograph after a painting/drawing, Johannes Gehrts 1901

Page 8 – Flammarion Woodcut, Artist unknown 1888

Page 10 – Nuremberg Chronicle, Hartmann Schedel 15th Century

Page 17 – Babylonian Inanna/Astarte, Nordisk Familjebok 1876

Page 27 – Izdubar and Heabani, artist unknown 1876

Page 34 – The angel of light in conflict with a dragon, Robert William Rogers 1908

Page 36 - Nut (sky) Geb (Earth) and Shu (Air), The gods of the Egyptians, E.A Wallace Budge 1904

Page 42 – The Egyptian Trinity – Isis, Osiris and Horus – Baedeker, Karl. Egypt, *Handbook for Traveling, pt.1 Lower Egypt, with the Fayum and the peninsula of Sinai.* K. Baedeker, Leipsic, 1885. p. 130.

Page 52 – The Olympian Gods, Nicolas-André Monsiau (1754-1837)

Page 54 – Fall of the Titans, Cornelis Cornelisz. van Haarlem, date unknown

Page 57 – The Midas Myth, A Wonder-Book for Girls and Boys. Illustration by Walter Crane, 1893

Page 60 – Greek god Dionysos - Stafylis date unknown

Page 74 – Pa - Shein – Eight Immortals in a temple in Hue, Vietnam

Page 83- Kuan Yin as sea goddess, von Günter Trageser date unknown

Page 85 – The Dragon, The Image and The Demon – The Three Religions of China - Hampden C Dubose 1887

Page 89 – Thor, Johannes Gehrts 1901

Page 90 – Frigga Spinning the Clouds, Guerber, H. A. (Hélène Adeline) 1909.

Page 93 – Ragnarok. Xylograph after a painting/drawing, Johannes Gehrts 1901

Page 95 – Freya in Dwarfs Cave, Illustration by Huard 1891

Page 104 – Freya's chariot drawn by cats. Manual of Mythology: Greek and Roman, Norse, and Old German, Hindoo and Egyptian Mythology. London, Asher and Co. This illustration is from plate XXXV Ludwig Pietsch 1865

Page 106 – Mural on Dublin Street, Desmond Kinney 1974

Page 112 – Macha Curses the Men of Ulster, Eleanor Hull 1902

Page 119 – Green Man Foliate head – UK © Copyright Richard Croft and licensed for reuse under Creative Commons Licence.

Page 123 – Fairy with wand, Open Clip Art Library 2013

Page 127 – Quetzalcoatl, God of Wisdom, Codex Borgia 16th Century

Page 130 – Aztec gods and goddess, Codex Laud 16th Century

Page 132 – Aztec Priest sacrifices victim, Codex Laud 16th century

Page 142 – Legba Loa Veve symbol, artist unknown

Page 146 – Erzulie as Black Madonna, Photograph of Black Madonna of Częstochowa

Page 150 – Damballah La Flambeau, Hector Hyppolite 1945

Page 152 – Veve or hand drawing of the Damballah Loa Symbol, artist unknown

Page 158 – A sketch of the eight Haitian Voodoo devotees found guilty in 1864 in the affaire de Bizoton, Artist unknown 1864

Page 159 – Congolese Nkondi Carving, artist unknown, held in Hood Museum of Art, Dartmouth College, Hanover, New Hampshire, USA.

Page 163 – Stonehenge sunrise ritual July 2013, Stonehenge Stone Circle group, Flickr Image used under creative commons

About the author

Gabiann Marin is an award-winning author, screenwriter, editor, academic and lover of all things Supernatural. Her very first stage play won the Australian Bicentennial Premier's prize and her book, *A True Person* won the international White Raven Literary award for work of outstanding merit and importance. She has written eight original works of fiction and non-fiction, many of which regularly appear on the Premier's reading lists across Australia.

When not writing, Gabiann runs a successful script and story development agency through which she has edited or helped develop over 200 books, screenplays, multimedia projects and stage plays. She also teaches writing and media courses at Macquarie University and the Australian Film Television and Radio School. Gabiann is currently completing her PhD on the role of the goddess in contemporary literature and working on her next novel featuring the Goddess Hera.

· MIDAS' DAUGHTER · TURNED · TO · GOLD ·